Houghton Mifflin
Mathematics

Practice

1

HOUGHTON MIFFLIN

BOSTON • MORRIS PLAINS, NJ

California • Colorado • Georgia • Illinois • New Jersey • Texas

Contents

Name _____ Date _____

Addition Concepts

You can use counters to find the numbers. Then write the numbers.

1.

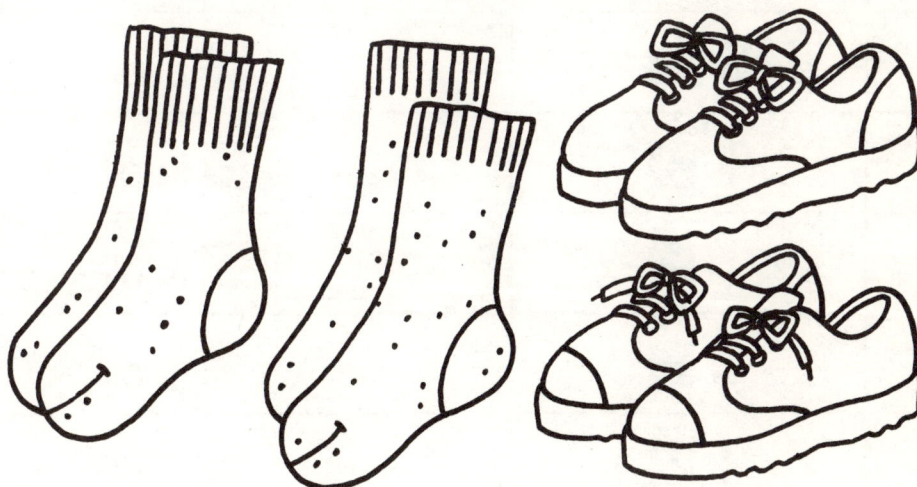

_____ pairs of socks _____ pairs of sneakers _____ pairs in all

2.

_____ coats _____ hats _____ in all

Name _____   Date _____

Model Addition

Write how many in all.

	Show	Add	How many in all?
1.	2 ■	3 ■	__5__ ■ in all
2.	3 ■	1 ■	_____ ■ in all
3.	1 ■	1 ■	_____ ■ in all
4.	2 ■	1 ■	_____ ■ in all
5.	1 ■	4 ■	_____ ■ in all
6.	3 ■	4 ■	_____ ■ in all
7.	2 ■	2 ■	_____ ■ in all

Problem Solving • Reasoning

8. Draw dots to show each number.
   Write how many in all.

   [ ]   [ ]

   4   and   2   _____ in all

Name _____ Date _____

Use Symbols to Add

Write how many in all.

1.

$$3 + 2 = \underline{5}$$

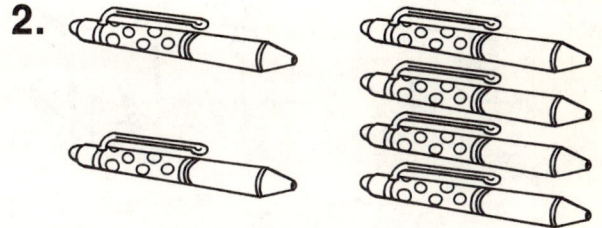

2.

$$2 + 4 = \underline{\quad}$$

3.

$$1 + 3 = \underline{\quad}$$

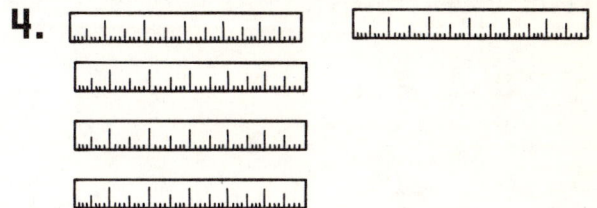

4.

$$4 + 1 = \underline{\quad}$$

Problem Solving • Reasoning

Visual Thinking

5. Circle the group that shows 2 + 3 = 5

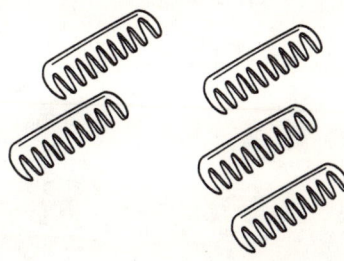

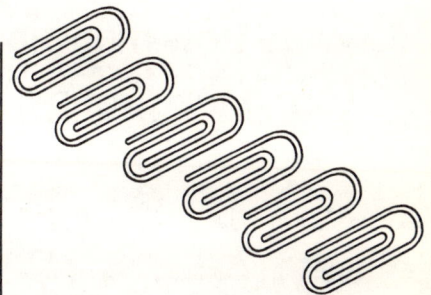

Name _____ Date _____

Write Addition Sentences

Write each addition sentence.

1.
2.

___2___ + ___3___ = ___5___   _____ + _____ = _____

Write each sum.

3. 3 + 3 = _____   4. 4 + 1 = _____   5. 2 + 2 = _____

6. 3 + 2 = _____   7. 3 + 1 = _____   8. 4 + 2 = _____

9. 1 + 5 = _____   10. 2 + 3 = _____   11. 1 + 1 = _____

12. 2 + 1 = _____   13. 1 + 3 = _____   14. 5 + 1 = _____

Problem Solving • Reasoning

15. Write how many in each group.
    Circle the group that has more.

 _____

 _____

Name _____   **Date** _____

Add With Zero

Write each sum.

1.

$$5 + 0 = \underline{5}$$

2.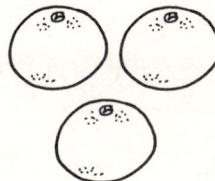

$$0 + 3 = \underline{}$$

3. $2 + 0 = \underline{}$ **4.** $6 + 0 = \underline{}$ **5.** $0 + 6 = \underline{}$

6. $4 + 1 = \underline{}$ **7.** $3 + 1 = \underline{}$ **8.** $1 + 2 = \underline{}$

9. $0 + 3 = \underline{}$ **10.** $3 + 3 = \underline{}$ **11.** $3 + 2 = \underline{}$

12. $3 + 0 = \underline{}$ **13.** $4 + 0 = \underline{}$ **14.** $0 + 0 = \underline{}$

Problem Solving • Reasoning

Write each addition sentence.

15. Three plus two equals five.

$$\underline{} + \underline{} = \underline{}$$

16. Four plus zero equals four.

$$\underline{} + \underline{} = \underline{}$$

Name _____   **Date** _____

Problem Solving: Use Models to Act It Out

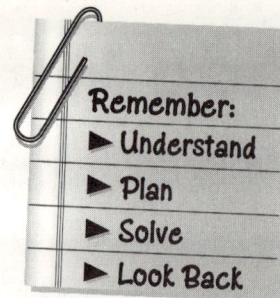

Remember:
► Understand
► Plan
► Solve
► Look Back

You can use models to act out problems.
Solve each problem using counters.

1. Sam has 1 shell. Then he found 3 more shells. How many shells does he have now?

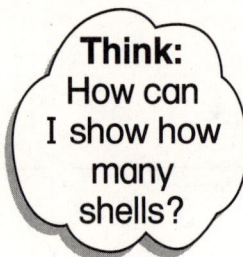

Think: How can I show how many shells?

Draw or write to explain.

_____ shells

2. Ann had 4 dollar bills. Her dad gave her 2 more. How many dollar bills does she have now?

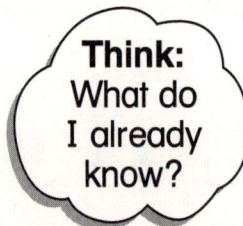

Think: What do I already know?

Draw or write to explain.

_____ dollar bills

Solve. Choose a strategy.

• Use models to act it out.
• Draw a picture.

3. Juan has 5 baseball cards. Marcos gives him 1 more. How many baseball cards does Juan have?

Draw or write to explain.

_____ baseball cards

Name _____ Date _____

Add in Any Order

Make a cube train using two colors. Then write
two addition sentences for each train.

1. Make a 5 train.

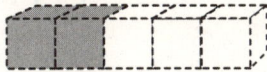

$2 + 3 = 5$

$3 + 2 = 5$

2. Make a 4 train.

___ + ___ = ___

___ + ___ = ___

Add. Then change the order and write a new
addition sentence.

3. $2 + 1 = $ ___

___ + ___ = ___

4. $4 + 0 = $ ___

___ + ___ = ___

5. $4 + 2 = $ ___

___ + ___ = ___

6. $1 + 5 = $ ___

___ + ___ = ___

Problem Solving • Reasoning

Algebra Readiness: Functions

For each number in the table,
use the rule at the top.

7.

Add 1	
1	2
4	
2	
5	

8.

Add 2	
0	2
4	
2	
1	

Name _____ Date _____

Ways to Make 7

Write each sum. Use cubes if you want.

1. 3 + 4 = ____   2. 3 + 1 = ____   3. 3 + 3 = ____

4. 3 + 0 = ____   5. 2 + 3 = ____   6. 2 + 4 = ____

7. 4 + 3 = ____   8. 1 + 6 = ____   9. 2 + 5 = ____

Add. Then write each fact another way.

10. 3 + 4 = ____   11. 2 + 5 = ____   12. 1 + 6 = ____

____ + ____ = ____ | ____ + ____ = ____ | ____ + ____ = ____

Problem Solving • Reasoning

Visual Thinking

13. Add 🐚 and 🐚 . Write how many in all.

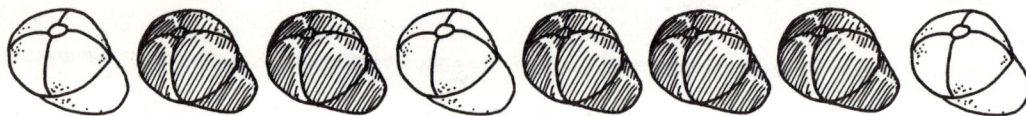

____ 🐚 + ____ 🐚 = ____ in all

Name _____   **Date** _____

Ways to Make 8

Add. Circle the problems that have the sum of 8.

1. (1 + 7) = _8_ | 2. 7 + 0 = ___ | 3. 3 + 5 = ___

4. 2 + 2 = ___ | 5. 5 + 1 = ___ | 6. 4 + 2 = ___

7. 3 + 3 = ___ | 8. 5 + 3 = ___ | 9. 3 + 1 = ___

10. 4 + 3 = ___ | 11. 8 + 0 = ___ | 12. 5 + 0 = ___

13. 6 + 2 = ___ | 14. 2 + 1 = ___ | 15. 0 + 8 = ___

16. 4 + 1 = ___ | 17. 7 + 1 = ___ | 18. 4 + 4 = ___

Name _____ Date _____

Algebra Readiness: The Equals Sign

Write each sum.

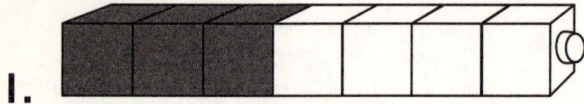

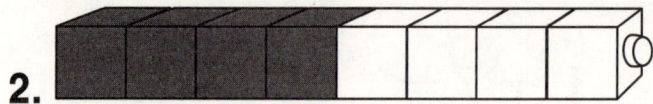

1. ____ = 3 + 4

2. ____ = 4 + 4

3. ____ = 3 + 2   4. ____ = 0 + 6   5. ____ = 2 + 2

6. ____ = 4 + 4   7. ____ = 4 + 1   8. ____ = 3 + 4

9. ____ = 1 + 6   10. ____ = 6 + 1   11. ____ = 1 + 4

12. 0 + 8 = ____   13. 3 + 2 = ____   14. 4 + 2 = ____

15. 2 + 4 = ____   16. 1 + 7 = ____   17. 5 + 2 = ____

Problem Solving • Reasoning

Write the missing number.

18. 4 + 1 = 1 + ____   19. 6 + 2 = 2 + ____

20. 5 + ____ = 3 + 5   21. ____ + 7 = 7 + 1

Name _____ Date _____

Add in Vertical Form

Write each addition fact.

1. $\begin{array}{r} 3 \\ + 4 \\ \hline 7 \end{array}$

2. $\begin{array}{r} \square \\ + \square \\ \hline \square \end{array}$

3. $\begin{array}{r} \square \\ + \square \\ \hline \square \end{array}$

4. $\begin{array}{r} 6 \\ +1 \\ \hline \end{array}$
5. $\begin{array}{r} 6 \\ +0 \\ \hline \end{array}$
6. $\begin{array}{r} 8 \\ +0 \\ \hline \end{array}$
7. $\begin{array}{r} 2 \\ +2 \\ \hline \end{array}$
8. $\begin{array}{r} 0 \\ +7 \\ \hline \end{array}$
9. $\begin{array}{r} 3 \\ +5 \\ \hline \end{array}$

10. $\begin{array}{r} 3 \\ +1 \\ \hline \end{array}$
11. $\begin{array}{r} 5 \\ +2 \\ \hline \end{array}$
12. $\begin{array}{r} 6 \\ +1 \\ \hline \end{array}$
13. $\begin{array}{r} 4 \\ +3 \\ \hline \end{array}$
14. $\begin{array}{r} 2 \\ +3 \\ \hline \end{array}$
15. $\begin{array}{r} 5 \\ +0 \\ \hline \end{array}$

Problem Solving • Reasoning

16. Write each sum. What addition fact likely comes next in this pattern?

$\begin{array}{r} 1 \\ +3 \\ \hline \end{array}$ $\begin{array}{r} 2 \\ +3 \\ \hline \end{array}$ $\begin{array}{r} 3 \\ +3 \\ \hline \end{array}$ $\begin{array}{r} 4 \\ +3 \\ \hline \end{array}$ $\begin{array}{r} \square \\ +\square \\ \hline \square \end{array}$

Name _____   Date _____

Problem Solving: Use Addition

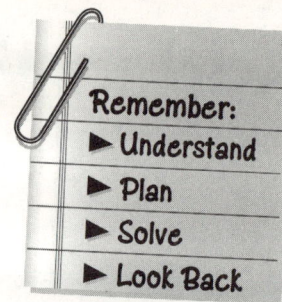

Solve. You can add to solve problems.

1. Last week it rained 3 days. This week it rained 2 days. How many days did it rain in all?

   Think: What do I need to find out?

   Draw or write to explain.

   _____ days

2. Last week it snowed 1 day. This week it snowed 2 days. How many days did it snow in all?

   Think: What should I do first?

   Draw or write to explain.

   _____ days

Solve. Choose a strategy.

• Use models to act it out.
• Draw a picture.

2. Last week it was sunny 4 days. This week it was sunny 3 days. How many sunny days were there in all?

   Draw or write to explain.

   _____ sunny days

Name _____   Date _____

Subtraction Concepts

Read the stories. Show each story with pictures. Write the numbers.

1. Tomas had 4 circles. He gave two circles to Pei. How many circles does Tomas have left?

_____ ◯   _____ given to Pei   _____ left

2. Malika had 5 triangles. She gave one triangle to each of her 4 friends. How many triangles does she have left?

_____ △   _____ given to friends   _____ left

Name _____ Date _____

Model Subtraction

Subtract. Write how many are left.

	Show	Take away.	How many are left?
1.	4 ■	2 ■	_2_ left
2.	5 ■	1 ■	____ left
3.	3 ■	3 ■	____ left
4.	5 ■	3 ■	____ left
5.	4 ■	1 ■	____ left
6.	2 ■	1 ■	____ left
7.	3 ■	2 ■	____ left

Problem Solving • Reasoning

Draw each group with 1 less.

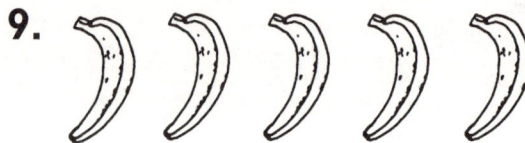

8.

9.

10. Explain how you know there is 1 less._____

Name _____ Date _____

Use Symbols to Subtract

Cross out to subtract. Write how many are left.

1.

$5 - 3 =$ __2__

2.

$4 - 1 =$ ____

3.

$6 - 2 =$ ____

4.

$7 - 3 =$ ____

5.
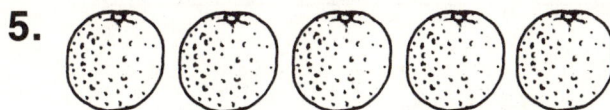

$5 - 4 =$ ____

6.
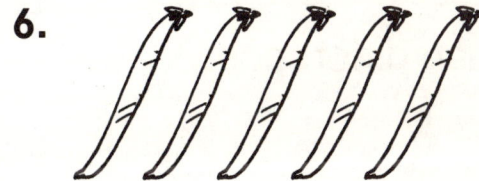

$5 - 2 =$ ____

Problem Solving • Reasoning

7. Circle the picture that shows $6 - 3 = 3$.

Name _____   Date _____

Write Subtraction Sentences

Write a subtraction sentence to show the difference.

1.

$\underline{\quad5\quad} - \underline{\quad2\quad} = \underline{\quad3\quad}$

2.

_____ – _____ = _____

3.

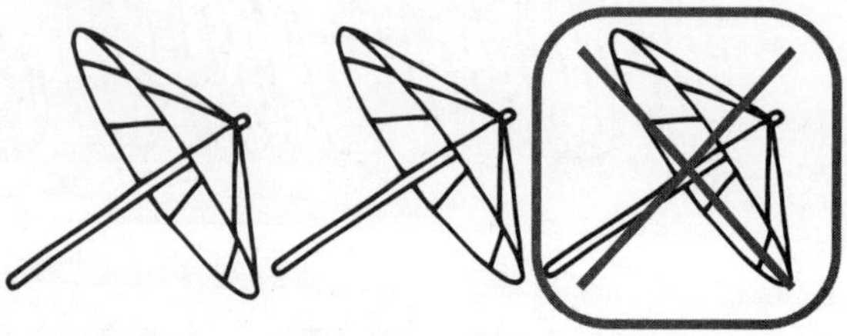

_____ – _____ = _____

4.

_____ – _____ = _____

Write each difference.

5. $6 - 3 =$ ____   6. $5 - 1 =$ ____   7. $4 - 2 =$ ____

8. $6 - 4 =$ ____   9. $3 - 1 =$ ____   10. $6 - 2 =$ ____

Problem Solving • Reasoning

11. I am greater than 2. I am less than 5. I am not 4. What number am I? ____

Draw or write to explain.

Name _____   **Date** _____

Zero in Subtraction

Find each difference.

1.

$4 - 4 = \underline{0}$

2.

$3 - 0 = \underline{}$

3.

$5 - 5 = \underline{}$

4.

$2 - 0 = \underline{}$

5. $3 - 0 = \underline{}$ | 6. $2 - 2 = \underline{}$ | 7. $4 - 0 = \underline{}$

8. $3 - 3 = \underline{}$ | 9. $5 - 0 = \underline{}$ | 10. $6 - 6 = \underline{}$

11. $2 - 0 = \underline{}$ | 12. $1 - 1 = \underline{}$ | 13. $6 - 0 = \underline{}$

Problem Solving • Reasoning

Write each subtraction sentence.

14. Five minus three equals two.

15. Four minus four equals zero.

____ – ____ = ____   ____ – ____ = ____

Name _____ Date _____

Problem Solving: Draw a Picture

You can draw pictures to help you solve problems.

Draw a picture to solve each problem.

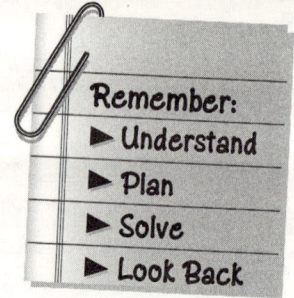

1. There are 2 baseballs in a bucket. Tom takes 1 of them. How many are left?

_____ baseball

Think: How many baseballs do I draw?

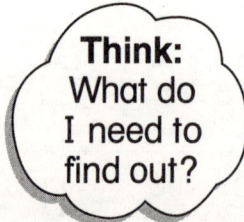

Draw or write to explain.

2. Sally has 4 pencils. She gives 2 away. How many pencils does she have left?

_____ pencils

Think: What do I need to find out?

Draw or write to explain.

Solve. Choose a strategy.

• Draw a picture.
• Use models to act it out.

3. Carlos grew 5 plants. He gave away 2 of them. How many plants are left?

_____ plants

Draw or write to explain.

Name _____ **Date** _____

Subtract From 7 or Less

Write each difference.

1. 6 − 3 = __3__ | 2. 5 − 4 = ____ | 3. 5 − 0 = ____

4. 6 − 1 = ____ | 5. 5 − 2 = ____ | 6. 4 − 0 = ____

7. 6 − 2 = ____ | 8. 6 − 6 = ____ | 9. 3 − 2 = ____

10. 4 − 3 = ____ | 11. 5 − 2 = ____ | 12. 4 − 4 = ____

Problem Solving • Reasoning

Write each subtraction sentence.

13. Tony had 7 🍎. He ate 6.

How many 🍎 are left?

____ − ____ = ____

| Draw or write to explain. |

14. Alexa has 7 🥕. She gives

2 to Tony. How many 🥕

does she have now?

____ − ____ = ____

| Draw or write to explain. |

Subtract From 8 or Less

Write each difference.

$8 - 0 =$ _____

$8 - 1 =$ _____

$8 - 2 =$ _____

$8 - 3 =$ _____ $7 - 0 =$ _____

$8 - 4 =$ _____ $7 - 1 =$ _____

$8 - 5 =$ _____ $7 - 2 =$ _____

$8 - 6 =$ _____ $7 - 3 =$ _____

$8 - 7 =$ _____ $7 - 4 =$ _____

$8 - 8 =$ _____ $7 - 5 =$ _____

$7 - 6 =$ _____

$7 - 7 =$ _____

Name _____ Date _____

Subtract in Vertical Form

Write each difference.

1. $\begin{array}{r} 7 \\ -0 \\ \hline 7 \end{array}$
2. $\begin{array}{r} 6 \\ -4 \\ \hline \end{array}$
3. $\begin{array}{r} 5 \\ -4 \\ \hline \end{array}$
4. $\begin{array}{r} 3 \\ -2 \\ \hline \end{array}$
5. $\begin{array}{r} 8 \\ -1 \\ \hline \end{array}$
6. $\begin{array}{r} 7 \\ -7 \\ \hline \end{array}$

7. $\begin{array}{r} 2 \\ -2 \\ \hline \end{array}$
8. $\begin{array}{r} 5 \\ -3 \\ \hline \end{array}$
9. $\begin{array}{r} 3 \\ -3 \\ \hline \end{array}$
10. $\begin{array}{r} 6 \\ -2 \\ \hline \end{array}$
11. $\begin{array}{r} 8 \\ -4 \\ \hline \end{array}$
12. $\begin{array}{r} 8 \\ -0 \\ \hline \end{array}$

13. $\begin{array}{r} 4 \\ -2 \\ \hline \end{array}$
14. $\begin{array}{r} 5 \\ -1 \\ \hline \end{array}$
15. $\begin{array}{r} 5 \\ -5 \\ \hline \end{array}$
16. $\begin{array}{r} 7 \\ -5 \\ \hline \end{array}$
17. $\begin{array}{r} 1 \\ -1 \\ \hline \end{array}$
18. $\begin{array}{r} 6 \\ -6 \\ \hline \end{array}$

Problem Solving • Reasoning

19. Write how many.
Then circle the
greater number.

_____   _____

Name _____ **Date** _____

Problem Solving: Choose the Operation

You can add or subtract to solve a problem.
Solve.

1. Michael writes 2 sentences. Then he writes 3 more. How many sentences did he write in all?

   Think: Do I add or subtract?

   Draw or write to explain.

   _____ sentences

2. Anna draws 4 pictures. She gives 2 away. How many pictures does Anna have now?

   Think: How many pictures does Anna have?

   Draw or write to explain.

   _____ pictures

Solve. Choose a strategy.

· Use models to act it out.
· Draw a picture.

3. There were 6 children at the party. 2 more came. How many children are at the party now?

   Draw or write to explain.

   _____ children

Name _____   Date _____

Count On to Add

Count on to add.

1.

$5 + 2 = \underline{7}$

2.

$3 + 3 = \underline{\hspace{1cm}}$

3. $8 + 2 = \underline{\hspace{1cm}}$ | 4. $7 + 1 = \underline{\hspace{1cm}}$ | 5. $8 + 1 = \underline{\hspace{1cm}}$

6. $4 + 3 = \underline{\hspace{1cm}}$ | 7. $2 + 3 = \underline{\hspace{1cm}}$ | 8. $5 + 3 = \underline{\hspace{1cm}}$

| 9. $\begin{array}{r} 3 \\ +2 \\ \hline \end{array}$ | 10. $\begin{array}{r} 7 \\ +3 \\ \hline \end{array}$ | 11. $\begin{array}{r} 2 \\ +1 \\ \hline \end{array}$ | 12. $\begin{array}{r} 0 \\ +1 \\ \hline \end{array}$ | 13. $\begin{array}{r} 3 \\ +1 \\ \hline \end{array}$ | 14. $\begin{array}{r} 4 \\ +1 \\ \hline \end{array}$ |

| 15. $\begin{array}{r} 6 \\ +3 \\ \hline \end{array}$ | 16. $\begin{array}{r} 2 \\ +2 \\ \hline \end{array}$ | 17. $\begin{array}{r} 6 \\ +1 \\ \hline \end{array}$ | 18. $\begin{array}{r} 5 \\ +1 \\ \hline \end{array}$ | 19. $\begin{array}{r} 9 \\ +1 \\ \hline \end{array}$ | 20. $\begin{array}{r} 0 \\ +2 \\ \hline \end{array}$ |

Problem Solving • Reasoning

21. How many [leaf] and [leaf] are there in all?

_____ in all

Name _____ **Date** _____

Add in Any Order

Start with the greater number. Count on to add.

1. $5 + 3 = \underline{8}$

   $3 + 5 = \underline{8}$

2. $1 + 3 = \underline{}$

   $3 + 1 = \underline{}$

3. $3 + 2 = \underline{}$

   $2 + 3 = \underline{}$

4. $6 + 3 = \underline{}$

   $3 + 6 = \underline{}$

5. $5 + 2 = \underline{}$

   $2 + 5 = \underline{}$

6. $2 + 1 = \underline{}$

   $1 + 2 = \underline{}$

7. $\begin{array}{r}4\\+2\\\hline\end{array}$ $\begin{array}{r}2\\+4\\\hline\end{array}$

8. $\begin{array}{r}4\\+1\\\hline\end{array}$ $\begin{array}{r}1\\+4\\\hline\end{array}$

9. $\begin{array}{r}7\\+1\\\hline\end{array}$ $\begin{array}{r}1\\+7\\\hline\end{array}$

10. $\begin{array}{r}8\\+2\\\hline\end{array}$ $\begin{array}{r}2\\+8\\\hline\end{array}$

11. $\begin{array}{r}9\\+1\\\hline\end{array}$ $\begin{array}{r}1\\+9\\\hline\end{array}$

12. $\begin{array}{r}4\\+3\\\hline\end{array}$ $\begin{array}{r}3\\+4\\\hline\end{array}$

Problem Solving • Reasoning

13. You start at 3. You end at 8. How many did you count on?

    _____

    Draw or write to explain.

Name _____ Date _____

Use a Number Line to Add

Start with the greater number. Write each sum.

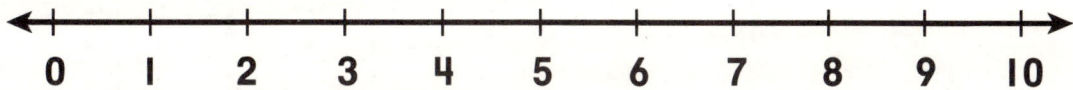

0 1 2 3 4 5 6 7 8 9 10

1. $5 + 1 = \underline{6}$ | 2. $6 + 3 = \underline{\quad}$ | 3. $3 + 2 = \underline{\quad}$

4. $4 + 3 = \underline{\quad}$ | 5. $1 + 8 = \underline{\quad}$ | 6. $1 + 2 = \underline{\quad}$

7. $\begin{array}{r} 6 \\ +1 \\ \hline \end{array}$
8. $\begin{array}{r} 8 \\ +2 \\ \hline \end{array}$
9. $\begin{array}{r} 1 \\ +7 \\ \hline \end{array}$
10. $\begin{array}{r} 4 \\ +1 \\ \hline \end{array}$
11. $\begin{array}{r} 2 \\ +6 \\ \hline \end{array}$
12. $\begin{array}{r} 4 \\ +2 \\ \hline \end{array}$

13. $\begin{array}{r} 2 \\ +3 \\ \hline \end{array}$
14. $\begin{array}{r} 1 \\ +3 \\ \hline \end{array}$
15. $\begin{array}{r} 7 \\ +2 \\ \hline \end{array}$
16. $\begin{array}{r} 3 \\ +7 \\ \hline \end{array}$
17. $\begin{array}{r} 7 \\ +2 \\ \hline \end{array}$
18. $\begin{array}{r} 1 \\ +7 \\ \hline \end{array}$

Problem Solving • Reasoning

Use the number line above.

19. What number is 3 more than 6? _____

20. What number is 1 more than 9? _____

21. What number is 2 more than 4? _____

Name _____ Date _____

Use Doubles to Add

Write each sum.

1.
$\begin{array}{r} 3 \\ +3 \\ \hline 6 \end{array}$ $\quad$ $\begin{array}{r} 3 \\ +4 \\ \hline 7 \end{array}$ $\quad$ $\begin{array}{r} 4 \\ +3 \\ \hline 7 \end{array}$

2.
$\begin{array}{r} 4 \\ +4 \\ \hline \end{array}$ $\quad$ $\begin{array}{r} 4 \\ +5 \\ \hline \end{array}$ $\quad$ $\begin{array}{r} 5 \\ +4 \\ \hline \end{array}$

3. $\begin{array}{r} 1 \\ +9 \\ \hline \end{array}$ 4. $\begin{array}{r} 8 \\ +2 \\ \hline \end{array}$ 5. $\begin{array}{r} 2 \\ +3 \\ \hline \end{array}$ 6. $\begin{array}{r} 2 \\ +2 \\ \hline \end{array}$ 7. $\begin{array}{r} 0 \\ +2 \\ \hline \end{array}$ 8. $\begin{array}{r} 1 \\ +8 \\ \hline \end{array}$

9. $\begin{array}{r} 2 \\ +7 \\ \hline \end{array}$ 10. $\begin{array}{r} 1 \\ +6 \\ \hline \end{array}$ 11. $\begin{array}{r} 5 \\ +0 \\ \hline \end{array}$ 12. $\begin{array}{r} 6 \\ +3 \\ \hline \end{array}$ 13. $\begin{array}{r} 5 \\ +5 \\ \hline \end{array}$ 14. $\begin{array}{r} 7 \\ +0 \\ \hline \end{array}$

15. $\begin{array}{r} 8 \\ +1 \\ \hline \end{array}$ 16. $\begin{array}{r} 2 \\ +5 \\ \hline \end{array}$ 17. $\begin{array}{r} 3 \\ +3 \\ \hline \end{array}$ 18. $\begin{array}{r} 3 \\ +5 \\ \hline \end{array}$ 19. $\begin{array}{r} 4 \\ +5 \\ \hline \end{array}$ 20. $\begin{array}{r} 4 \\ +1 \\ \hline \end{array}$

Problem Solving • Reasoning

Choose a number to make each double fact.

21. $\begin{array}{r} 5 \\ +\ \square \\ \hline 10 \end{array}$ 22. $\begin{array}{r} 3 \\ +\ 3 \\ \hline \square \end{array}$ 23. $\begin{array}{r} \square \\ +\ 4 \\ \hline 8 \end{array}$

6 3

4 5

Name _____ Date _____

Draw a Picture to Add

Draw a picture for each addition sentence.
Write each sum.

1.
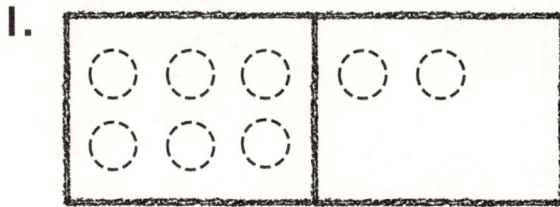

$6 + 2 = \underline{8}$

2.

$5 + 3 = \underline{}$

Write each sum. Draw a picture to help if you want.

3.	9 +1	4.	4 +3	5.	1 +7	6.	6 +3	7.	4 +6	8.	3 +6

9.	2 +5	10.	5 +3	11.	4 +4	12.	6 +4	13.	8 +2	14.	3 +3

Problem Solving • Reasoning

Answer each question.

$$6 + 4 = 10$$

15. The **sum** is _____.

16. The **addends** are _____ and _____.

17. The **greater** addend is _____.

Name _____   Date _____

Different Ways to Add

Choose a way to add. Write each sum.

1. 2
   +8

   10

2. 1
   +6

3. 7
   +3

4. 5
   +5

5. 1
   +8

6. 2
   +7

7. 3
   +4

8. 4
   +3

9. 3
   +6

10. 10
    + 0

11. 9 + 0 = _____   12. 7 + 2 = _____   13. 3 + 5 = _____

Problem Solving · Reasoning

14. Use the clues to find each house. Write
    the correct letter under each house.

    House A has ⊞.   House B has ⊞⊞.

    House C has a ⌐.   House D has a ▭▭▭.

Name _____   **Date** _____

Count Back to Subtract

Count back to subtract.

1.

$8 - 2 = \underline{6}$

2.

$10 - 3 = \underline{}$

3. $5 - 1 = \underline{}$ | 4. $8 - 3 = \underline{}$ | 5. $4 - 2 = \underline{}$

6. $7 - 2 = \underline{}$ | 7. $1 - 1 = \underline{}$ | 8. $7 - 1 = \underline{}$

9.
$$\begin{array}{r} 10 \\ -\ 1 \\ \hline \end{array}$$
10.
$$\begin{array}{r} 6 \\ -2 \\ \hline \end{array}$$
11.
$$\begin{array}{r} 8 \\ -3 \\ \hline \end{array}$$
12.
$$\begin{array}{r} 7 \\ -3 \\ \hline \end{array}$$
13.
$$\begin{array}{r} 1 \\ -0 \\ \hline \end{array}$$
14.
$$\begin{array}{r} 3 \\ -2 \\ \hline \end{array}$$

15.
$$\begin{array}{r} 4 \\ -1 \\ \hline \end{array}$$
16.
$$\begin{array}{r} 2 \\ -2 \\ \hline \end{array}$$
17.
$$\begin{array}{r} 10 \\ -\ 3 \\ \hline \end{array}$$
18.
$$\begin{array}{r} 9 \\ -2 \\ \hline \end{array}$$
19.
$$\begin{array}{r} 5 \\ -3 \\ \hline \end{array}$$
20.
$$\begin{array}{r} 10 \\ -\ 2 \\ \hline \end{array}$$

Problem Solving • Reasoning

21. Greg has 6 grapes. He eats 4.
    How many grapes does he have left?

    _____ grapes

    > Draw or write to explain.

Name _____ Date _____

Use a Number Line to Subtract

Use the number line to count back. Write each
difference.

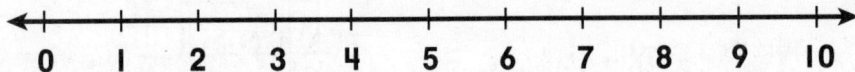

0 1 2 3 4 5 6 7 8 9 10

1. 9
   −3
    6

2. 2
   −1

3. 5
   −2

4. 7
   −3

5. 10
   − 3

6. 7
   −2

7. 5
   −1

8. 8
   −3

9. 10
   − 1

10. 4
    −2

11. 4
    −3

12. 8
    −2

13. 6
    −2

14. 9
    −2

15. 5
    −3

Problem Solving • Reasoning

16. Josh has 8 apple slices. He gives 3 to
    Matt. How many apple slices does Josh
    have left?

    _____ − _____ = _____

Name _____ **Date** _____

Draw a Picture to Subtract

Draw a picture for each subtraction sentence.
Cross out. Write each difference.

1.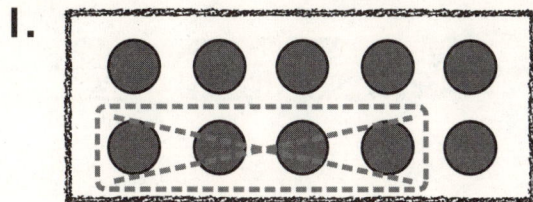

$10 - 4 = \underline{6}$

2.

$8 - 5 = \underline{}$

Write each difference. Draw a picture to help if you want.

3.	4.	5.	6.	7.	8.
8 − 6	5 − 3	10 − 7	6 − 3	9 − 7	7 − 5

9.	10.	11.	12.	13.	14.
7 − 7	6 − 5	7 − 6	8 − 4	6 − 1	10 − 6

Problem Solving • Reasoning

15. John has 10 cans of paint. He uses 6 of them. How many cans are left?

Draw or write to explain.

_____ cans

Name _____   **Date** _____

Subtract to Compare

Match. Then subtract.

1. How many more 🐰 than 🥕?

🐰 🐰 🐰 🐰 🐰 🐰 🐰 🐰 🐰 🐰

🥕 🥕 🥕 🥕 🥕

$10 - 5 =$ ___5___

2. How many more 🐕 than 🦴?

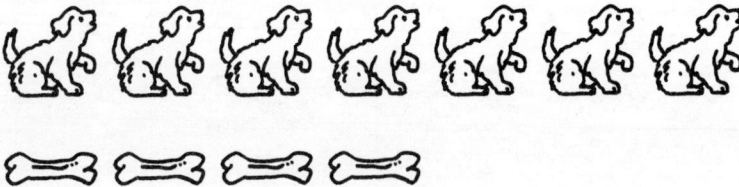

🐕 🐕 🐕 🐕 🐕 🐕 🐕

🦴 🦴 🦴 🦴

$7 - 4 =$ _____

Problem Solving • Reasoning

3. Jen has 5 flowers. She picks 4 more. How many flowers does Jen have in all?

   _____ flowers

Draw or write to explain.

Name _____   **Date** _____

Problem Solving: Use Subtraction

You can subtract to find out how many are left.
You can subtract to compare numbers.
Subtract.

1. 9 elephants were standing
   by the river. 7 elephants
   walked away. How many
   elephants were left?

   Think: What numbers do I subtract?

   Draw or write to explain.

   _____ elephants

2. 6 monkeys were climbing
   trees. There were 3 trees.
   How many more monkeys
   were there than trees?

   Think: How can I find out how many more?

   Draw or write to explain.

   _____ more monkeys

Solve. Choose a strategy.

• Use models to act it out.
• Draw a picture.

3. 6 tigers were eating dinner. 4 tigers
   left to play. How many tigers were
   still eating?

   Draw or write to explain.

   _____ tigers

Name _____   Date _____

Algebra Readiness: Relate Addition and Subtraction

Add or subtract. Use cubes if you want.

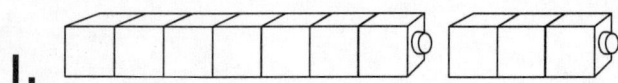

1. $7 + 3 = \underline{10}$

   $10 - 3 = \underline{7}$

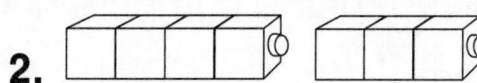

2. $4 + 3 = \underline{}$

   $7 - 4 = \underline{}$

3.
$$\begin{array}{r} 2 \\ +4 \\ \hline \end{array} \qquad \begin{array}{r} 6 \\ -4 \\ \hline \end{array}$$

4.
$$\begin{array}{r} 6 \\ +4 \\ \hline \end{array} \qquad \begin{array}{r} 10 \\ -\ 4 \\ \hline \end{array}$$

5.
$$\begin{array}{r} 4 \\ +4 \\ \hline \end{array} \qquad \begin{array}{r} 8 \\ -4 \\ \hline \end{array}$$

6.
$$\begin{array}{r} 6 \\ +3 \\ \hline \end{array} \qquad \begin{array}{r} 9 \\ -3 \\ \hline \end{array}$$

7.
$$\begin{array}{r} 2 \\ +6 \\ \hline \end{array} \qquad \begin{array}{r} 8 \\ -6 \\ \hline \end{array}$$

8.
$$\begin{array}{r} 3 \\ +7 \\ \hline \end{array} \qquad \begin{array}{r} 10 \\ -\ 7 \\ \hline \end{array}$$

Problem Solving • Reasoning

Find the difference. Circle the related addition fact.

9.
$$\begin{array}{r} 10 \\ -\ 7 \\ \hline \end{array}$$
$6 + 3 = 9$
$3 + 7 = 10$

10.
$$\begin{array}{r} 9 \\ -6 \\ \hline \end{array}$$
$3 + 6 = 9$
$4 + 6 = 10$

Name _____ **Date** _____

Fact Families

Use a workmat and cubes to show each fact.

Write each fact family.

1.

Whole	
10	
Part	Part
4	6

$4 + 6 = 10$ | $10 - 6 = 4$

___ + ___ = ___ | ___ - ___ = ___

2.

Whole	
8	
Part	Part
5	3

___ + ___ = ___ | ___ - ___ = ___

___ + ___ = ___ | ___ - ___ = ___

3.

Whole	
7	
Part	Part
3	4

___ + ___ = ___ | ___ - ___ = ___

___ + ___ = ___ | ___ - ___ = ___

Problem Solving • Reasoning

Choose the number that is the missing addend.

4 5 6 7

4. $10 = \boxed{} + 5$

5. $8 = \boxed{} + 2$

6. $10 = \boxed{} + 6$

Name _____ **Date** _____

Different Ways to Subtract

Choose a way to subtract.
Write each difference.

1. $4 - 2 =$ __2__   2. $9 - 4 =$ ___   3. $9 - 8 =$ ___

4.
$$\begin{array}{r} 10 \\ -\ 6 \\ \hline \end{array}$$
5.
$$\begin{array}{r} 5 \\ -\ 4 \\ \hline \end{array}$$
6.
$$\begin{array}{r} 2 \\ -\ 0 \\ \hline \end{array}$$
7.
$$\begin{array}{r} 8 \\ -\ 3 \\ \hline \end{array}$$
8.
$$\begin{array}{r} 10 \\ -\ 8 \\ \hline \end{array}$$
9.
$$\begin{array}{r} 9 \\ -\ 5 \\ \hline \end{array}$$

10.
$$\begin{array}{r} 7 \\ -\ 7 \\ \hline \end{array}$$
11.
$$\begin{array}{r} 10 \\ -\ 0 \\ \hline \end{array}$$
12.
$$\begin{array}{r} 4 \\ -\ 3 \\ \hline \end{array}$$
13.
$$\begin{array}{r} 10 \\ -\ 5 \\ \hline \end{array}$$
14.
$$\begin{array}{r} 8 \\ -\ 8 \\ \hline \end{array}$$
15.
$$\begin{array}{r} 6 \\ -\ 0 \\ \hline \end{array}$$

16.
$$\begin{array}{r} 3 \\ -\ 1 \\ \hline \end{array}$$
17.
$$\begin{array}{r} 9 \\ -\ 6 \\ \hline \end{array}$$
18.
$$\begin{array}{r} 8 \\ -\ 1 \\ \hline \end{array}$$
19.
$$\begin{array}{r} 5 \\ -\ 3 \\ \hline \end{array}$$
20.
$$\begin{array}{r} 10 \\ -\ 7 \\ \hline \end{array}$$
21.
$$\begin{array}{r} 7 \\ -\ 1 \\ \hline \end{array}$$

Problem Solving • Reasoning

Use the clues to find the number.

22. I am at the end of a row.
I am not inside a circle.
I am less than 5.
I am greater than 2.
Which number am I? _____

6 ⑤ 3
⑧ 7 ②
1 ⑨ 10

Name _____   Date _____

Problem Solving: Write a Number Sentence

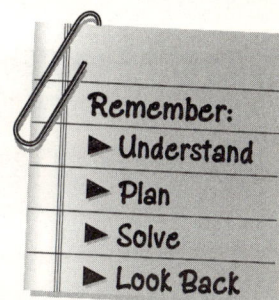

You can write a number sentence to help you solve problems.

Solve. Write a number sentence.

1. One bell rang 2 times. Another bell rang 4 times. How many times did the bells ring in all?

Think: Do I need to add or subtract?

Draw or write to explain.

_____ ◯ _____ = _____ times

2. A whistle blew 5 times. A horn beeped 2 times. How many more whistles than beeps were there?

Think: Do I need to add or subtract?

Draw or write to explain.

_____ more whistles

Solve. Choose a strategy.

• Write a number sentence.
• Draw a picture.

3. One owl hooted 6 times. One owl did not hoot at all. How many hoots were there altogether?

Draw or write to explain.

_____ hoots

Name _____   Date _____

Sorting Objects

Circle all the shapes that belong in each group.

1. Squares

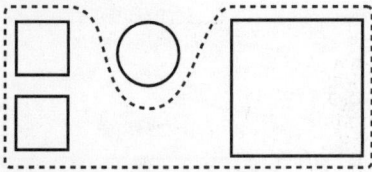

2. Large shapes

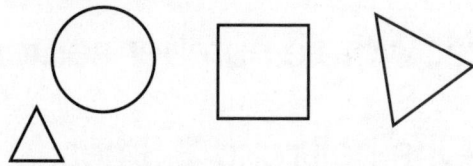

3. Small shapes

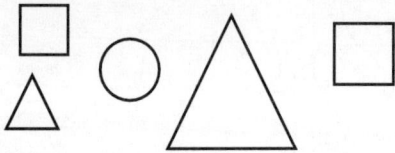

4. Dark shapes

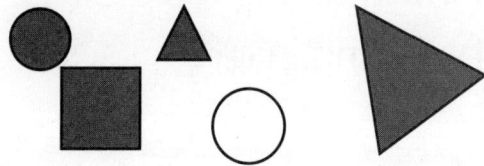

5. Light shapes

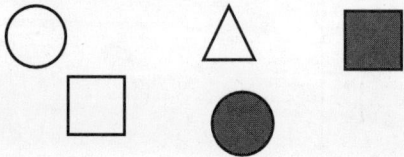

6. Circles

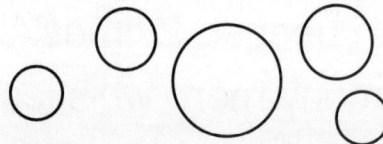

Problem Solving • Reasoning

Draw what likely comes next in the pattern.

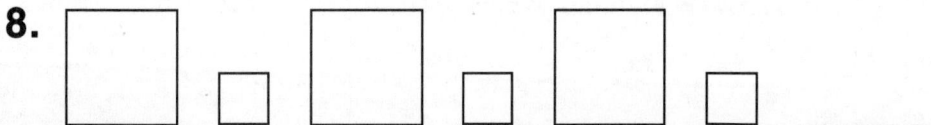

7. ___

8. ___

Name _____ **Date** _____

Make a Tally Chart

Use the picture to complete the tally chart.

Animals	Tally	Total
🐘	‖	2
🐅		
🐒		
🐦		

Use your chart.

1. Circle the one that has 5.

2. How many giraffes are there?

_____

3. Circle the one that has the least.

4. Circle the one that has 6.

5. Show the tally marks for the number 10.

Name _____   Date _____

Read a Picture Graph

Use the graph to answer the questions below.

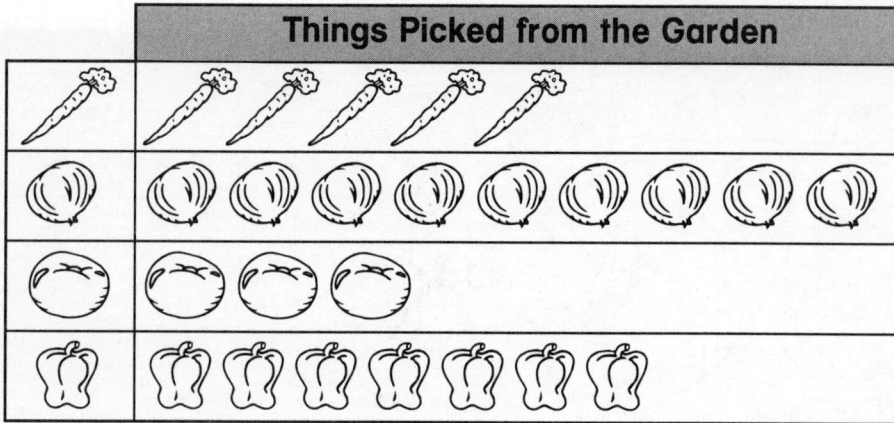

| Things Picked from the Garden | | | | | | | | | |

1. How many 🥕 and 🍅 are there?

   __8__ in all

2. How many more 🧅 than 🫑 are there?

   _____ more

3. Circle the one that has the most.

   🧅   🫑   🍅

4. How many fewer 🧅 than 🥕 are there?

   _____ fewer

Problem Solving • Reasoning

Write the number sentence.

5. There are 6 🍅. Neal picks 4. How many 🍅 are left?

   _____ ◯ _____ = _____

Name _____ Date _____

Make a Picture Graph

Use the picture to make a graph. Color to show how many.

	On the Pizza									
🍕	◯	◯	◯	◯	◯	◯	◯	◯	◯	◯
🍄	🍄	🍄	🍄	🍄	🍄	🍄	🍄	🍄	🍄	🍄
🥦	🥦	🥦	🥦	🥦	🥦	🥦	🥦	🥦	🥦	🥦

Use the picture graph.

1. How many fewer 🥦 than 🍄 are there?

_____ fewer

2. How many more ◯ than 🥦 are there?

_____ more

Problem Solving • Reasoning

Make a picture graph.

3. There are 5 ✏️.

There is 1 less ✏️ than 🖊️.

There are 2 more ✏️ than 🖍️.

	Things We Use to Write
✏️	
🖊️	
🖍️	

Name _____ Date _____

Problem Solving: Use Logical Thinking

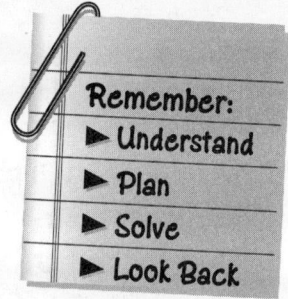

You can use clues to help you solve problems.
Solve. Circle the one that matches the clues.

1. It has 4 legs.
   It lives in a house.

   Think: Which ones have 4 legs?

2. It has 2 legs.
   It can walk and fly.

   Think: Which ones do not walk?

Solve. Choose a strategy.

- Use logical thinking.
- Use models to act it out.
- Draw a picture.

3. 9 horses ran in races at the fair.
   3 more horses ran in the second
   race than in the first race. How
   many horses ran in each race?

   Draw or write to explain.

   _____ horses ran in the first race.

   _____ horses ran in the second race.

Name _____ **Date** _____

Read a Bar Graph

This graph shows the fruit people ate for lunch.

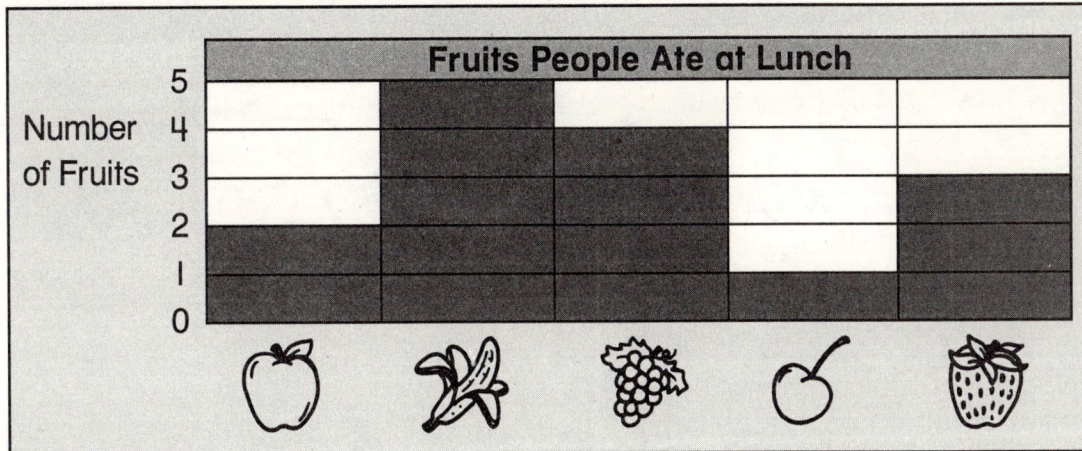

Fruits People Ate at Lunch

Number of Fruits: 5 4 3 2 1 0

Use the bar graph.

1. How many fewer 🍒 than 🍓 were eaten?

   __2__ fewer

2. How many 🍎 and 🍓 in all?

   _____ in all

3. Circle the one that was eaten the most.

4. Circle the one that was eaten the least.

Problem Solving • Reasoning

Show the tally marks for each number.

5. _____ seven

6. _____ sixteen

7. _____ twelve

Name _____ Date _____

Make a Bar Graph

Use the picture to make a bar graph.

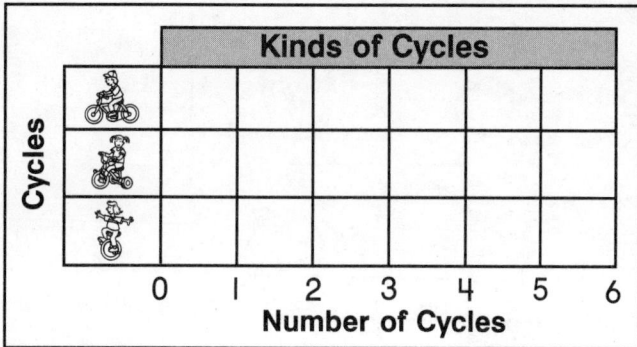

Kinds of Cycles

Cycles

0 1 2 3 4 5 6
Number of Cycles

Use the bar graph.

1. Circle the one that has the most.

2. Circle the one that has 3 more than .

3. Make a bar graph.
Show that there are 3 .

There are 3 more than .

There are 4 fewer than .

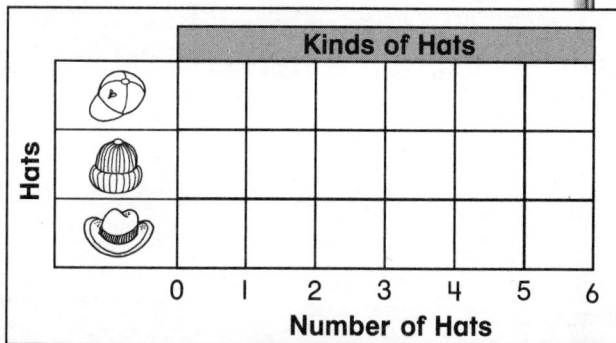

Kinds of Hats

Hats

0 1 2 3 4 5 6
Number of Hats

Name _____ **Date** _____

Different Ways to Show Data

Use the tally chart. Make a bar graph.

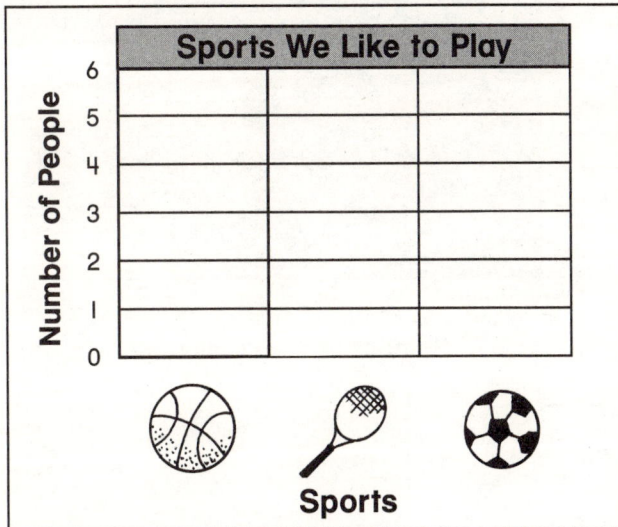

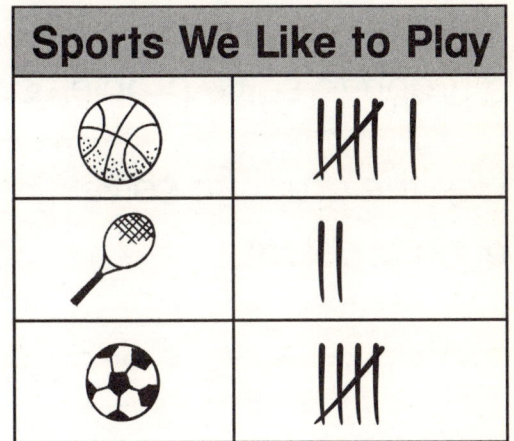

Sports We Like to Play

🏀	IIII I
🎾	II
⚽	IIII

Sports We Like to Play

Number of People: 6 5 4 3 2 1 0

Sports

Use the bar graph.
Circle each answer.

1. Which sport has more?

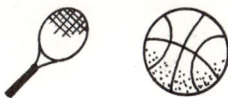

2. Which sport has 4 more than 🎾 ?

Write Your Own

3. Write a question about this graph.

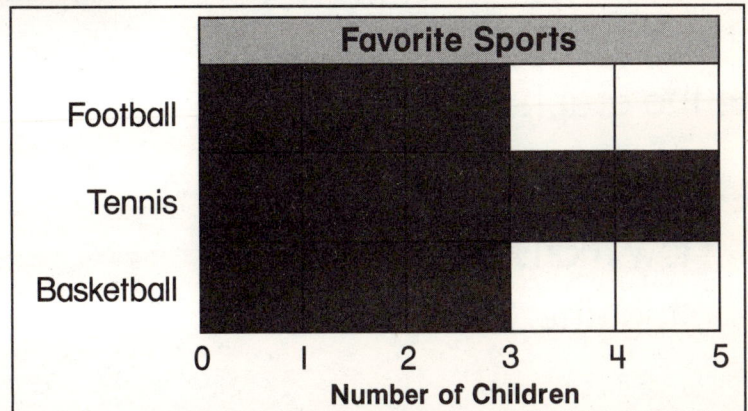

Favorite Sports

Football
Tennis
Basketball

0 1 2 3 4 5
Number of Children

Name _____ Date _____

Problem Solving: Use a Bar Graph

You can use the data from a graph to solve problems.

Use the graph to solve each problem.

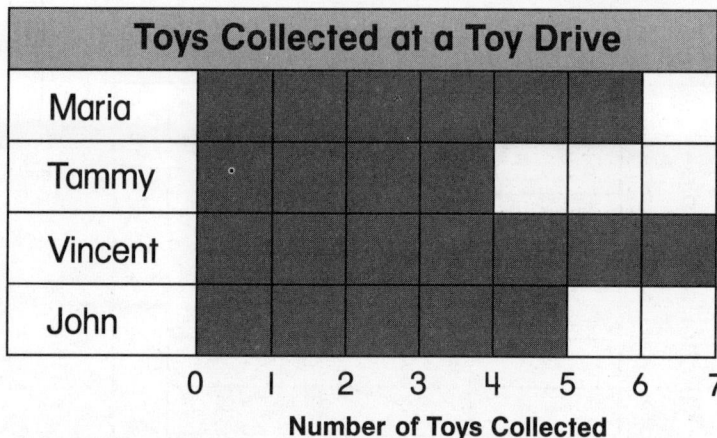

Toys Collected at a Toy Drive							
Maria							
Tammy							
Vincent							
John							

0 1 2 3 4 5 6 7
Number of Toys Collected

1. How many toys did Tammy and John collect together?

   Think: Which numbers should I use?

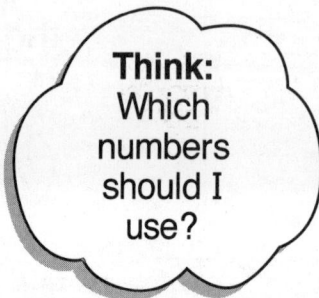

   Draw or write to explain.

   _____ toys

2. How many more toys did Maria collect than John?

   Think: Which numbers should I use?

   Draw or write to explain.

   _____ more toy

Solve. Choose a strategy. Use the graph.

- Use models to act it out.
- Write a number sentence.
- Draw a picture.

3. Tammy collected 3 more toys. How many did she collect altogether?

   Draw or write to explain.

   _____ toys

Name _____ Date _____

Teen Numbers

Write each number.

1. _16_

2. ____

3. ____

4. ____

5. ____

6. ____

Write the missing numbers.

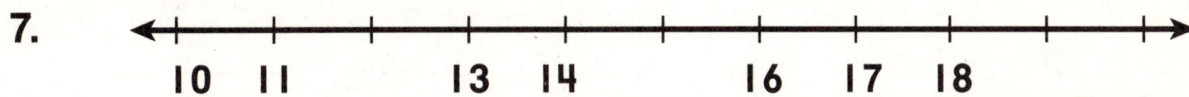

7.

10 11 ____ 13 14 ____ 16 17 18 _____

8. ____, ____, 15, 16, 17

9. 20, 19, 18, ____,

Problem Solving • Reasoning

10. Write each number.
Explain why this is a pattern for teen numbers.

10 and 3 = ____, 10 and 4 = ____,

10 and 5 = ____, 10 and 6 = ____,

____ and ____ = ____, ____ and ____ = ____,

____ and ____ = ____

Name _____   Date _____

Count by Tens

Write each number.

1.

____8____ tens = __80__

2.

____ tens = ____

3.

____ tens = ____

4.

____ tens = ____

Write the missing numbers.

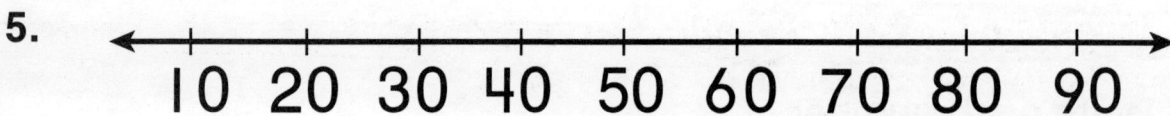

5.

10 20 30 40 50 60 70 80 90

10, 20, ____, 40, 50, ____, 70, ____, ____

Problem Solving • Reasoning

6. There are 10 crayons in one row. How many crayons are there in 3 rows?

Draw or write to explain.

____ crayons

Name _____   Date _____

Tens and Ones

Write the missing numbers.

	Show this many.	Regroup. Write the tens and ones.		Write the number.
1.	14 ones	__1__ ten	__4__ ones	__14__
2.	23 ones	_____ tens	_____ ones	_____
3.	16 ones	_____ ten	_____ ones	_____
4.	26 ones	_____ tens	_____ ones	_____
5.	21 ones	_____ tens	_____ one	_____
6.	27 ones	_____ tens	_____ ones	_____
7.	22 ones	_____ tens	_____ ones	_____
8.	25 ones	_____ tens	_____ ones	_____

Problem Solving • Reasoning

9. Circle the word name that is the same as
   1 ten 4 ones.

   sixteen   thirteen   fourteen

Name _____ Date _____

Numbers to 50

Write each number. Use ▭▭▭▭▭▭ and ▯
if you want.

1.
Tens	Ones
4	7

4̶7̶
forty-seven

2.
Tens	Ones
3	5

_____
thirty-five

3.
Tens	Ones
3	0

_____
thirty

4.
Tens	Ones
4	2

_____
forty-two

5.
Tens	Ones
4	8

_____
forty-eight

6.
Tens	Ones
3	2

_____
thirty-two

7.
Tens	Ones
3	9

_____
thirty-nine

8.
Tens	Ones
4	9

_____
forty-nine

9.
Tens	Ones
4	0

_____
forty

Problem Solving • Reasoning

Patterns

Write the missing numbers.

10. 45 = ___ and ___

55 = ___ and ___

65 = ___ and ___

75 = ___ and ___

11. 41 = ___ and ___

42 = ___ and ___

43 = ___ and ___

44 = ___ and ___

Name _____ **Date** _____

Numbers to 99

Write how many.

1.

Tens	Ones
7	2

_72_ seventy-two

2.

Tens	Ones

_____ eighty-four

3.

Tens	Ones

ninety-seven

4.

Tens	Ones

_____ sixty-six

Problem Solving • Reasoning

5. One feather starfish has 10 arms. How many arms will 8 feather starfish have?

_____ arms

Name _____ Date _____

One Hundred

Write how many.

1.

_____ tens _____ ones

_____

one hundred

2.

_____ tens _____ ones

_____

one hundred

Problem Solving • Reasoning

3. Lea has 6 boxes of beads. There are
   10 beads in each box. How many beads
   in all?

   _____ tens _____ beads in all

4. There are 2 rows of boxes. 5 boxes are in
   each row. Each box has 10 toys in it. How
   many toys in all?

   _____ tens _____ toys in all

Name _____   Date _____

Different Ways to Show Numbers

Write each number.

1. __3__ tens __7__ ones | __30__ + __7__

2. ____ tens ____ ones | ____ + ____

3. ____ tens ____ ones | ____ + ____

4. ____ tens ____ ones | ____ + ____

Problem Solving • Reasoning

5. Circle the name for the number.

60 + 70   6 + 7   60 + 7

67

Name _____ Date _____

Count by Twos

1. Write the missing numbers.

2. Count by twos. Draw an **X** through the numbers you counted.

2	3	4			7		9	10
11		13				17	18	19	20
			24		26	27			
31	32	33			36	37	38	39	40
	42	43	44	45	46	47	48		
51		53		55	56	57	58		60
61	62	63	64	65	66	67	68	69	70
71	72		74	75					80
81	82	83		85	86	87			90
91		93							100

Problem Solving • Reasoning

3. Each bird has 2 legs.
   There are 18 legs.
   How many birds are there?

   _____ birds

> Draw or write to explain.

Name _____ Date _____

Count by Fives

1. Write the missing numbers.

2. Count by fives. Color the numbers you counted.

3. Count by tens. Circle the tens.

1	2	3	4	5	6	7	8	9	10
11	12	13	14		16	17	18	19	
21	22	23	24		26	27	28	29	
31	32	33	34		36	37	38	39	
41	42	43	44		46	47	48	49	
51	52	53	54		56	57	58	59	
61	62	63	64		66	67	68	69	
71	72	73	74		76	77	78	79	
81	82	83	84		86	87	88	89	
91	92	93	94		96	97	98	99	

Problem Solving • Reasoning

4. Write the mystery number.

It is less than 80.

It is greater than 70.

You say it when counting by fives.

What number is it? _____

Draw or write to explain.

Name _____ **Date** _____

Number Patterns

Write the number that is
1 more.

1	2	3	4	5	6	7	8	9	10
11	12	13	14	15	16	17	18	19	20
21	22	23	24	25	26	27	28	29	30
31	32	33	34	35	36	37	38	39	40
41	42	43	44	45	46	47	48	49	50

1. | 38 | 39 |

2. | | |

3. | 44 | |

4. | 31 | |

Write the number that is 10 more.

5. 9

6. 37

7. 11

8. 23

Write the number that is 10 less.

9. 39

10. 15

11. 43

12. 30

Problem Solving • Reasoning

13. Follow the pattern on a hundred chart. Write the missing numbers.

72		74	
81	82		
		96	97

Name _____ **Date** _____

Ordinal Numbers

Color.

1.

first - yellow   fourth - purple   seventh - red
second - blue   fifth - orange   eighth - green

Problem Solving • Reasoning

2. Find the fourth 🐬. Count 1 more.
Color it blue.

3. Find the eighth 🐬. Count back 2.
Color it red.

Name _____ **Date** _____

Problem Solving: Find a Pattern

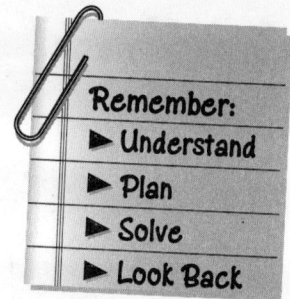

Solve. Find the pattern.

Remember:
► Understand
► Plan
► Solve
► Look Back

1. One cat has 4 legs. How many legs do 4 cats have?

   Think: What do I already know?

I cat	2 cats	3 cats	4 cats
4			

   4 cats have _____ legs

---

2. One book has 2 covers. How many covers do 3 books have?

   Think: How many covers do I add for each book?

I book	2 books	3 books

   3 books have _____ covers

Solve. Choose a strategy.

• Draw a picture.
• Write a number sentence.

3. One building has 3 doors. How many doors are in 3 buildings?

   3 buildings have _____ doors.

   Draw or write to explain.

Name _____ **Date** _____

Use Ten to Estimate

Circle one group of ten. Estimate. Then count.

1.

Estimate
40
Count
37

2.

Estimate
____
Count
____

Problem Solving • Reasoning

Use the graph.
Write how many of each.

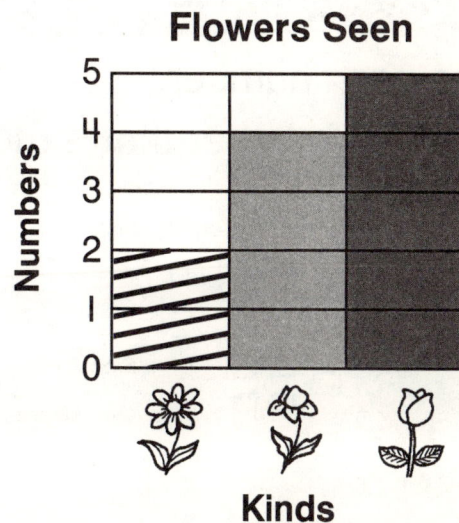

Flowers Seen

3. 🌼 _____

4. 🌸 _____

5. 🌷 _____

Name _____   **Date** _____

Compare Numbers

Circle the number that is greater.

1.   56   (62)   **2.**   71   17

3.   95   59   **4.**   22   44

Circle the number that is less.

5.   85   86   **6.**   54   45

Problem Solving • Reasoning

7. Write each number.
   Circle the number that is more.

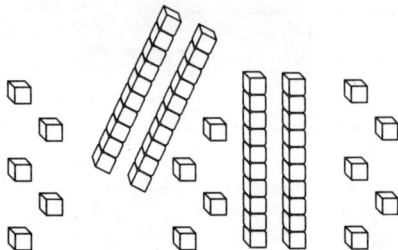   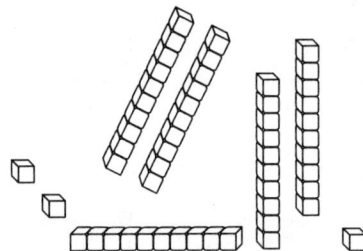

_____   _____

Name _____ Date _____

Use Symbols to Compare Numbers

Compare. Circle >, <, or =.

1. (45) >   (48)
   =
   (<)

2. (80) >   (77)
   =
   <

3. (19) >   (19)
   =
   <

4. (99) >   (66)
   =
   <

5. (35) >   (41)
   =
   <

6. (54) >   (45)
   =
   <

Problem Solving • Reasoning

7. Circle the ways that show 43.

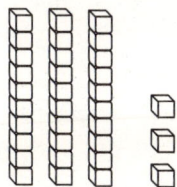 | 40 + 3 | 4 tens 3 ones |

Name _____ Date _____

Order Numbers

Write each number that comes **before** or **after**.

1. _45_, 46 | 2. ___, 28 | 3. ___, 11

4. 55, ___ | 5. ___, 39 | 6. 90, ___

Write the number that comes **between.**

7. 19, ___, 21 | 8. 95, ___, 97 | 9. 31, ___, 33

10. 79, ___, 81 | 11. 17, ___, 19 | 12. 69, ___, 71

Write the missing numbers.

13. 74, ___, ___, 77 | 14. 53, ___, ___, 56

| Problem Solving • Reasoning |

15. Bill has 20 shells.
He finds 20 more.
He gives 10 to Kate.
How many shells does Bill
have now?

Draw or write to explain.

_____ shells

Name _____ Date _____

Problem Solving: Too Much Information

Cross out the information you do not need. Solve.

1. Three seals are swimming. One seal is still a pup. Three more seals join them. How many seals are there now?

   Think: What do I need to find out?

   _____ seals

   Draw or write to explain.

2. There are 7 sea lions lying on the beach. Three are asleep. Two sea lions swim away. How many sea lions are lying on the beach?

   Think: What information do I need?

   _____ sea lions

   Draw or write to explain.

Solve. Choose a strategy.

• Write a number sentence.
• Use models to act it out.

3. There are 7 jellyfish floating together in the ocean. 5 more jellyfish join them. How many jellyfish are floating together now?

   _____ jellyfish

   Draw or write to explain.

Name _____   Date _____

Count On to Add

Write each sum.

Use the number line if you want.

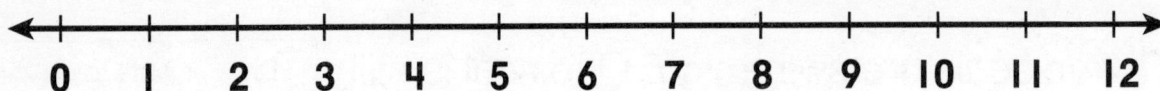

1. $4 + 4 =$ _8_ | 2. $8 + 1 =$ ___ | 3. $3 + 6 =$ ___

4. $3 + 5 =$ ___ | 5. $5 + 5 =$ ___ | 6. $2 + 5 =$ ___

7. $7 + 2 =$ ___ | 8. $4 + 5 =$ ___ | 9. $3 + 3 =$ ___

10. $4 + 2 =$ ___ | 11. $2 + 4 =$ ___ | 12. $7 + 0 =$ ___

13. $3 + 4 =$ ___ | 14. $7 + 3 =$ ___ | 15. $6 + 4 =$ ___

16. $2 + 3 =$ ___ | 17. $2 + 8 =$ ___ | 18. $9 + 2 =$ ___

19. $9 + 1 =$ ___ | 20. $1 + 6 =$ ___ | 21. $3 + 6 =$ ___

Problem Solving • Reasoning

22. Sarita and Jed saw
5 lions and 6 baby lions.
How many lions did
they see in all?   _____ lions

Name _____   **Date** _____

Sums to 11

Write each sum.

1.
$$\begin{array}{r} 6 \\ +5 \\ \hline 11 \end{array} \qquad \begin{array}{r} 5 \\ +6 \\ \hline 11 \end{array}$$

2.
$$\begin{array}{r} 5 \\ +4 \\ \hline \end{array} \qquad \begin{array}{r} 4 \\ +5 \\ \hline \end{array}$$

3.
$$\begin{array}{r} 7 \\ +3 \\ \hline \end{array} \qquad \begin{array}{r} 3 \\ +7 \\ \hline \end{array}$$

4.
$$\begin{array}{r} 7 \\ +4 \\ \hline \end{array} \qquad \begin{array}{r} 4 \\ +7 \\ \hline \end{array}$$

5.
$$\begin{array}{r} 6 \\ +2 \\ \hline \end{array} \qquad \begin{array}{r} 2 \\ +6 \\ \hline \end{array}$$

6.
$$\begin{array}{r} 9 \\ +2 \\ \hline \end{array} \qquad \begin{array}{r} 2 \\ +9 \\ \hline \end{array}$$

7.
$$\begin{array}{r} 4 \\ +2 \\ \hline \end{array} \qquad \begin{array}{r} 2 \\ +4 \\ \hline \end{array}$$

8.
$$\begin{array}{r} 11 \\ +\ 0 \\ \hline \end{array} \qquad \begin{array}{r} 0 \\ +11 \\ \hline \end{array}$$

9.
$$\begin{array}{r} 5 \\ +3 \\ \hline \end{array} \qquad \begin{array}{r} 3 \\ +5 \\ \hline \end{array}$$

10. $10 + 0 =$ ____   11. $7 + 4 =$ ____   12. $8 + 1 =$ ____

Problem Solving • Reasoning

Write each sum.

13.

____ $= 9 + 2$

14.

____ $= 3 + 7$

Name _____   Date _____

Sums to 12

Write each sum.

1.
$$\begin{array}{r} 2 \\ +10 \\ \hline 12 \end{array} \quad \begin{array}{r} 10 \\ +\ 2 \\ \hline 12 \end{array}$$

2.
$$\begin{array}{r} 7 \\ +2 \\ \hline \end{array} \quad \begin{array}{r} 2 \\ +7 \\ \hline \end{array}$$

3.
$$\begin{array}{r} 6 \\ +3 \\ \hline \end{array} \quad \begin{array}{r} 3 \\ +6 \\ \hline \end{array}$$

4.
$$\begin{array}{r} 6 \\ +5 \\ \hline \end{array} \quad \begin{array}{r} 5 \\ +6 \\ \hline \end{array}$$

5.
$$\begin{array}{r} 11 \\ +\ 1 \\ \hline \end{array} \quad \begin{array}{r} 1 \\ +11 \\ \hline \end{array}$$

6.
$$\begin{array}{r} 5 \\ +4 \\ \hline \end{array} \quad \begin{array}{r} 4 \\ +5 \\ \hline \end{array}$$

7.
$$\begin{array}{r} 7 \\ +5 \\ \hline \end{array} \quad \begin{array}{r} 5 \\ +7 \\ \hline \end{array}$$

8.
$$\begin{array}{r} 7 \\ +3 \\ \hline \end{array} \quad \begin{array}{r} 3 \\ +7 \\ \hline \end{array}$$

9.
$$\begin{array}{r} 9 \\ +1 \\ \hline \end{array} \quad \begin{array}{r} 1 \\ +9 \\ \hline \end{array}$$

10. $5 + 7 =$ _____
    $7 + 5 =$ _____

11. $3 + 9 =$ _____
    $9 + 3 =$ _____

12. $8 + 4 =$ _____
    $4 + 8 =$ _____

Problem Solving • Reasoning

13. **Write Your Own** Write a story about the pictures. Then write a number sentence.

_____ ◯ _____ = _____

Name _____ Date _____

Add Three Numbers

Write each sum.

1. 3
    4
  + 4
  ‾‾‾
    11

2. 6
    3
  + 2

3. 1
    4
  + 5

4. 2
    1
  + 6

5. 1
    1
  + 8

6. 1
    8
  + 3

7. 1
    7
  + 4

8. 4
    2
  + 5

9. 1
    0
  + 6

10. 5
    3
  + 1

11. 2
    8
  + 2

12. 3
    3
  + 3

13. 5
    6
  + 1

14. 2
    2
  + 4

15. 3
    3
  + 1

16. 7
    1
  + 1

17. 6
    2
  + 2

18. 4
    5
  + 3

Problem Solving • Reasoning

19. Fill in the ◯ with the numbers
    5, 6, or 8.
    The sum of each side
    should equal 11.

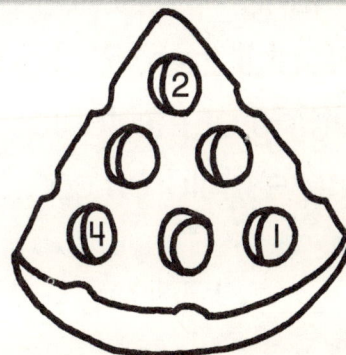

Name _____   Date _____

Algebra Readiness:
Missing Addends

Find each missing addend.
Use cubes if you want.

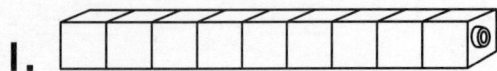

1. $\boxed{3} + 6 = 9$

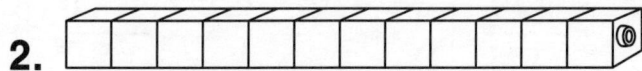

2. $5 + \boxed{} = 12$

3. $3 + \boxed{} = 11$ | 4. $2 + \boxed{} = 10$ | 5. $\boxed{} + 3 = 7$

6.
$$\begin{array}{r} 6 \\ + \boxed{} \\ \hline 11 \end{array}$$

7.
$$\begin{array}{r} 7 \\ + \boxed{} \\ \hline 10 \end{array}$$

8.
$$\begin{array}{r} \boxed{} \\ + \ 2 \\ \hline 12 \end{array}$$

9.
$$\begin{array}{r} \boxed{} \\ + \ 3 \\ \hline 9 \end{array}$$

10.
$$\begin{array}{r} 6 \\ + \boxed{} \\ \hline 8 \end{array}$$

Problem Solving • Reasoning

11. A lunch table has chairs for 12 children. 7 children are sitting at the table. How many more children can sit on chairs?

_____ children

Draw or write to explain.

Name _____ **Date** _____

Problem Solving: Make a Table

You can make a table to help you solve problems.

Coin	Number
Pennies	
Nickels	
Dimes	5

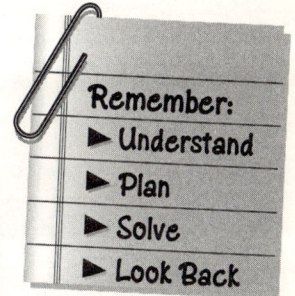

Remember:
► Understand
► Plan
► Solve
► Look Back

Solve. Complete the table.

1. There are 3 fewer pennies than dimes. How many pennies are there?

   Think: Do I add or subtract?

   Draw or write to explain.

   _____ pennies

2. There are 5 more nickels than dimes. How many nickels are there?

   Think: What numbers do I use?

   Draw or write to explain.

   _____ nickels

Solve. Choose a strategy.

• Make a table.
• Write a number sentence.

3. Use the table. How many more nickels are there than pennies?

   Draw or write to explain.

   _____ nickels

Count Back to Subtract

Subtract.
Use the number line if you want.

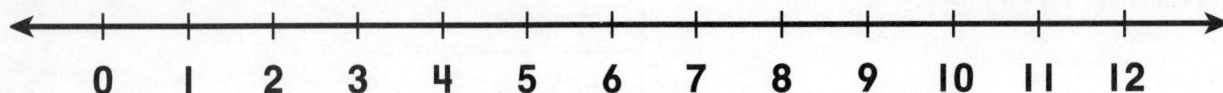

1. $9 - 3 = \underline{6}$
2. $12 - 6 = \underline{}$
3. $8 - 6 = \underline{}$

4. $11 - 6 = \underline{}$
5. $9 - 4 = \underline{}$
6. $10 - 3 = \underline{}$

7. $4 - 2 = \underline{}$
8. $7 - 5 = \underline{}$
9. $9 - 6 = \underline{}$

10. $6 - 2 = \underline{}$
11. $10 - 5 = \underline{}$
12. $7 - 2 = \underline{}$

Problem Solving • Reasoning

Write About it

13. Write a subtraction question that you can answer by using this graph.

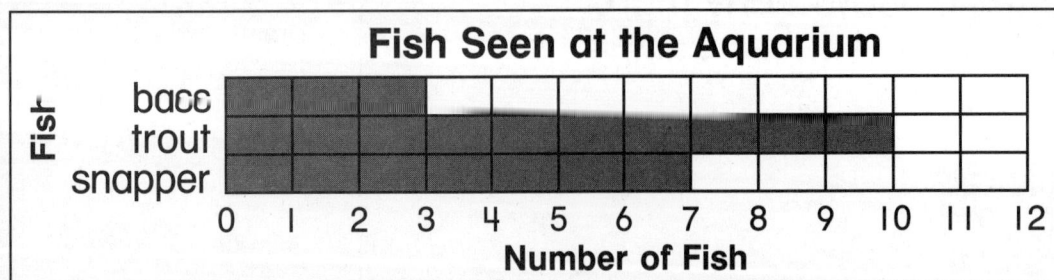

Fish Seen at the Aquarium

Fish / bass / trout / snapper / Number of Fish

0 1 2 3 4 5 6 7 8 9 10 11 12

Copyright © Houghton Mifflin Company. All rights reserved.

70 Use with text pages 267–268.

Practice 6-7

Name _____   Date _____

Subtract From 11 and Less

Write each difference.

1.
$$
\begin{array}{r} 11 \\ -\ 5 \\ \hline 6 \end{array}
\qquad
\begin{array}{r} 11 \\ -\ 6 \\ \hline 5 \end{array}
$$

2.
$$
\begin{array}{r} 9 \\ -7 \\ \hline \end{array}
\qquad
\begin{array}{r} 9 \\ -2 \\ \hline \end{array}
$$

3.
$$
\begin{array}{r} 10 \\ -\ 3 \\ \hline \end{array}
\qquad
\begin{array}{r} 10 \\ -\ 7 \\ \hline \end{array}
$$

4.
$$
\begin{array}{r} 11 \\ -\ 9 \\ \hline \end{array}
\qquad
\begin{array}{r} 11 \\ -\ 2 \\ \hline \end{array}
$$

5.
$$
\begin{array}{r} 11 \\ -\ 7 \\ \hline \end{array}
\qquad
\begin{array}{r} 11 \\ -\ 4 \\ \hline \end{array}
$$

6.
$$
\begin{array}{r} 9 \\ -3 \\ \hline \end{array}
\qquad
\begin{array}{r} 9 \\ -6 \\ \hline \end{array}
$$

7.
$$
\begin{array}{r} 10 \\ -\ 9 \\ \hline \end{array}
\qquad
\begin{array}{r} 10 \\ -\ 1 \\ \hline \end{array}
$$

8.
$$
\begin{array}{r} 8 \\ -2 \\ \hline \end{array}
\qquad
\begin{array}{r} 8 \\ -6 \\ \hline \end{array}
$$

9.
$$
\begin{array}{r} 11 \\ -\ 8 \\ \hline \end{array}
\qquad
\begin{array}{r} 11 \\ -\ 3 \\ \hline \end{array}
$$

10. $10 - 2 = $ _____

$10 - 8 = $ _____

11. $9 - 6 = $ _____

$9 - 3 = $ _____

Problem Solving • Reasoning

12. What number would you subtract from eleven to get a difference of five?

_____

13. Write two addends that have a sum of eleven.

_____ and _____

Name _____ Date _____

Subtract From 12 and Less

Write each difference.

1.
```
 12    12
- 3   - 9
 9     3
```

2.
```
 11    11
- 2   - 9
```

3.
```
 10    10
- 4   - 6
```

4.
```
 11    11
- 4   - 7
```

5.
```
  8     8
- 3   - 5
```

6.
```
 10    10
- 8   - 2
```

7. $11 - 5 =$ ____

   $11 - 6 =$ ____

8. $9 - 8 =$ ____

   $9 - 1 =$ ____

Problem Solving • Reasoning

Follow the rule to find each difference.

9.
Subtract 5	
12	7
11	
10	

10.
Subtract 4	
6	
7	
8	

11.
Subtract 3	
11	
10	
9	

Name _____   Date _____

Algebra Readiness:
Relate Addition and Subtraction

Solve.

1.
```
  6   11
+ 5 - 6
 11    5
```

2.
```
  3   12
+ 9 - 3
```

3.
```
  7   11
+ 4 - 7
```

4.
```
  2   10
+ 8 - 2
```

5.
```
  5    9
+ 4 - 5
```

6.
```
  6   12
+ 6 - 6
```

7.
```
  8   12
+ 4 - 8
```

8.
```
  3   10
+ 7 - 3
```

9.
```
  2    7
+ 5 - 2
```

10.
```
  5   12
+ 7 - 5
```

11.
```
  2   12
+10 - 2
```

12.
```
  8   11
+ 3 - 8
```

13.
```
  9   11
+ 2 - 9
```

14.
```
  7   14
+ 7 - 7
```

15.
```
 10   12
+ 2 -10
```

Name _____   Date _____

Algebra Readiness:
Fact Families for 11

Complete each fact family.

1.

$$7 + 4 = \underline{11}$$

$$4 + 7 = \underline{11}$$

$$11 - 7 = \underline{4}$$

$$11 - 4 = \underline{7}$$

2.

$$3 + 6 = \underline{}$$

$$6 + 3 = \underline{}$$

$$9 - 3 = \underline{}$$

$$9 - 6 = \underline{}$$

Problem Solving • Reasoning

Write About it

3. Pilar says she can make 4 groups of 3 nickels. Is she right? Explain.

_____

_____

Name _____   Date _____

Algebra Readiness:
Fact Families for 12

Add or subtract. Write the missing fact.

1.
12	
9	3

$9 + 3 = \underline{12}$ $12 - 9 = \underline{}$

$12 - 3 = \underline{}$ $\underline{} \bigcirc \underline{} = \underline{}$

2.
12	
2	10

$2 + 10 = \underline{}$ $12 - 2 = \underline{}$

$10 + 2 = \underline{}$ $\underline{} \bigcirc \underline{} = \underline{}$

3.
10	
6	4

$10 - 6 = \underline{}$ $10 - 4 = \underline{}$

$6 + 4 = \underline{}$ $\underline{} \bigcirc \underline{} = \underline{}$

Problem Solving • Reasoning

Complete each fact family.

4. $8 + 4 = \underline{}$

$\underline{} \bigcirc \underline{} = \underline{}$

$\underline{} \bigcirc \underline{} = \underline{}$

$\underline{} \bigcirc \underline{} = \underline{}$

5. $11 - 6 = \underline{}$

$\underline{} \bigcirc \underline{} = \underline{}$

$\underline{} \bigcirc \underline{} = \underline{}$

$\underline{} \bigcirc \underline{} = \underline{}$

Name _____   Date _____

Names for Numbers

Circle the names for each number on the left.

1. **7**	4 + 4	(11 − 4)	(2 + 2 + 3)
	(3 + 4)	10 − 5	4 + 2 + 2
2. **11**	5 + 6	7 + 4	0 + 6 + 6
	11 + 2	7 − 4	2 + 6 + 3
3. **6**	2 + 3	8 − 2	1 + 2 + 3
	5 + 1	4 + 3	3 + 1 + 3
4. **12**	6 + 6	7 + 3	3 + 3 + 3
	12 − 0	11 − 4	4 + 4 + 4

Problem Solving • Reasoning

5. Write each sum. Look for a pattern.
   Write the facts likely to come next.

```
  11     10      9      8      ☐      ☐
+  0   +  1    + 2    + 3    + ☐    + ☐
```

Name _____ **Date** _____

Problem Solving: Choose the Operation

Write the number sentence.
Add or subtract to solve.

1. Sid is making a photo album. He puts 6 photos on one page and 2 on another. How many photos has he placed in the book so far?

Think: Do I need to add or subtract?

Draw or write to explain.

_____ photos

2. Sid takes 3 pictures on Monday and 9 pictures on Thursday. How many more pictures did he take on Thursday than on Monday?

Think: Do I need to add or subtract?

Draw or write to explain.

_____ pictures

Solve. Choose a strategy.

• Choose the operation.
• Use logical thinking.
• Draw a picture.

3. The first page of the album has 5 pictures on it. Sid takes 3 of them off. How many pictures are left on the page?

Draw or write to explain.

_____ pictures

Name _____   Date _____

Value of Coins

Circle the coins to match each price.

1.

    10¢

2.

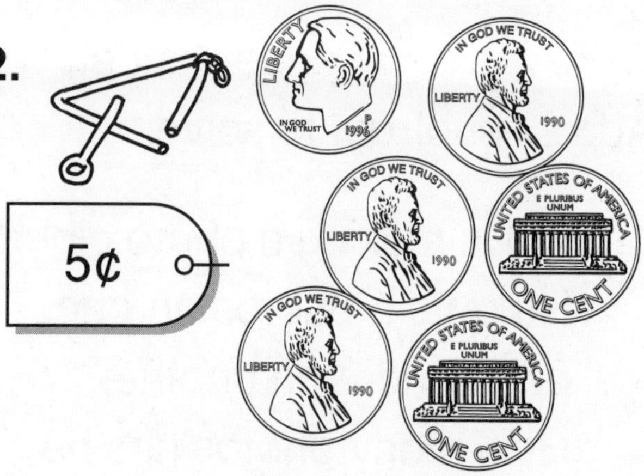

    5¢

3.

    10¢

4.

    10¢

Problem Solving • Reasoning

Write About It

5. Look at the picture. James has two nickels and 4 pennies. Circle the toys he can buy. Explain.

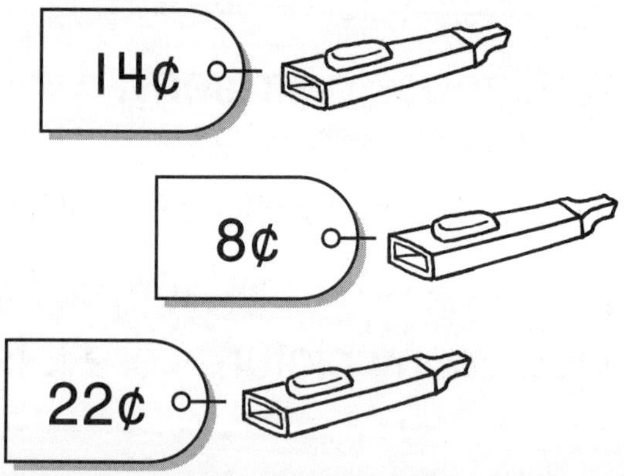

    14¢

    8¢

    22¢

Name _____ Date _____

Nickels

Count by fives. Write how much in all.

1.   $\underline{10}$¢
   in all

   $\underline{5}$ ¢ $\underline{10}$¢

2.       ____¢
   in all

   ____¢ ____¢ ____¢ ____¢

3.       ____¢
   in all

   ____¢ ____¢ ____¢ ____¢ ____¢ ____¢

Problem Solving • Reasoning

4. Jane counts her money like this: 5¢, 10¢,
   15¢, 20¢, 25¢, 30¢, 35¢, 40¢, 45¢.
   How many nickels does she have?

   _____ nickels

Name _____   Date _____

Nickels and Pennies

Circle the coins to match the price.

1. 16¢

2. 21¢

3. 8¢

4. 12¢

Problem Solving • Reasoning

5. A magazine costs 37¢. Circle the coins you need to pay for the magazine.

Name _____ **Date** _____

Dimes

Count by tens. Write how much in all.

1.

$\underline{10}$¢ $\underline{20}$¢ $\underline{30}$¢ $\underline{40}$¢

$\boxed{40}$¢

2.

____¢ ____¢ ____¢ ____¢ ____¢ ____¢ ____¢

$\boxed{}$¢

3.

____¢ ____¢ ____¢ ____¢ ____¢ ____¢

$\boxed{}$¢

Problem Solving • Reasoning

4. Cindy has 30¢. Her grandma gave her some dimes. Now she has 70¢. How much money did her grandma give her?

30¢ + ____ ¢ = 70¢

Draw or write to explain.

Name _____   Date _____

Dimes and Pennies

Circle the coins that match each price.

1.

2.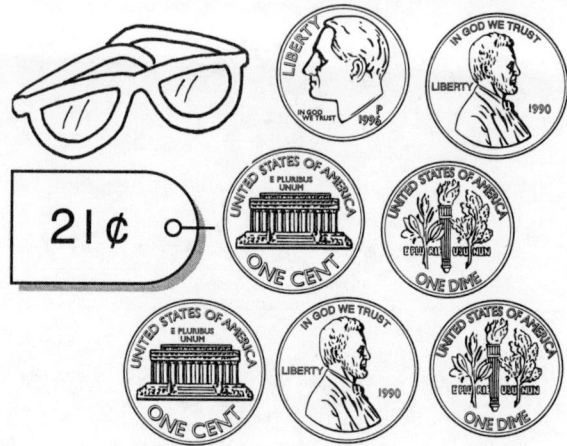

3.

4.

Problem Solving • Reasoning

5. Each child has 23¢. Write the number of
   coins each child has.

   Jill has 5 coins. _____ pennies _____ nickels _____ dimes

   Mike has 6 coins. _____ pennies _____ nickels _____ dimes

Name _____ Date _____

Count Coins

Write each amount.

1. 34¢

2. ____¢

3. ____¢

4. ____¢

Problem Solving • Reasoning

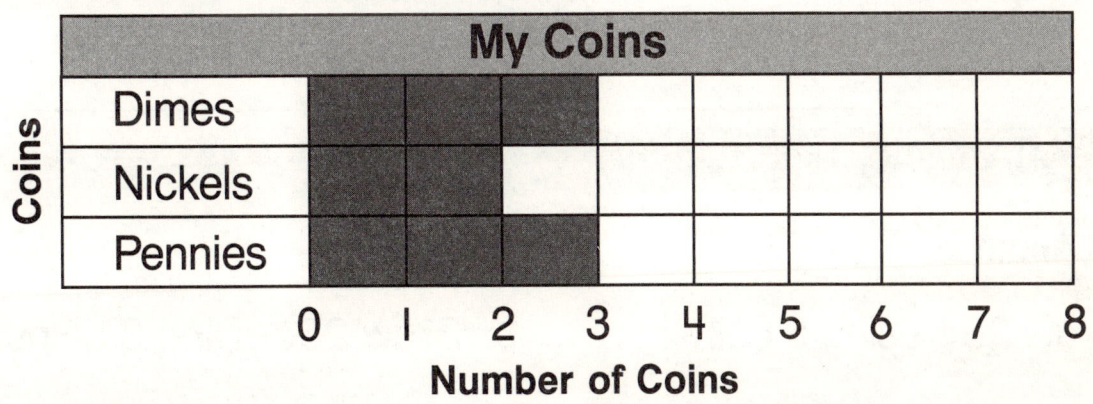

My Coins

Coins									
Dimes									
Nickels									
Pennies									

0   1   2   3   4   5   6   7   8

Number of Coins

5. **Write Your Own** Use this graph to write
   a word problem.

Name _____   Date _____

Equal Amounts

Draw two ways to make each amount.

1. 12¢

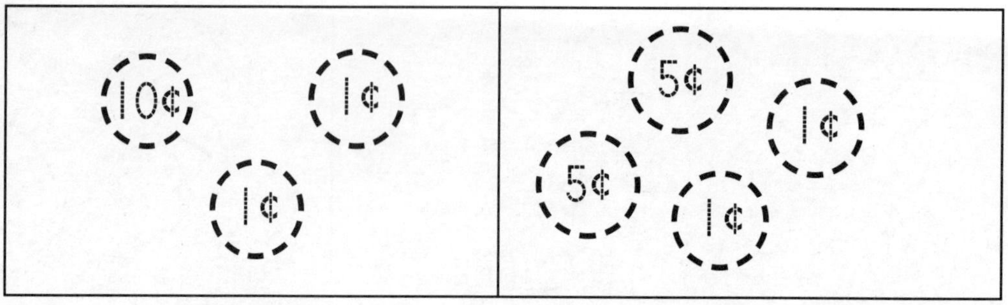

10¢   1¢   1¢   5¢   5¢   1¢   1¢

2. 21¢

3. 36¢

Problem Solving • Reasoning

Write About It

4. Draw 25¢ using 5 coins.   5. Draw 25¢ using 3 coins.

Explain.

Name _____ **Date** _____

Problem Solving: Use Models to Act It Out

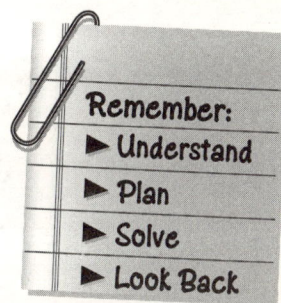

Solve. Use coins if you want.

1. Jacob bought a baseball card for 23 cents. He used 6 coins. What were they?

   Think: How can I solve the problem?

   Draw or write to explain.

   _____

2. Jessica wanted 25 cents to buy a pack of gum. Her mother gave her 4 nickels for cleaning the car. She had 8 pennies. Can she buy the gum? Explain.

   Think: How much money does she have?

   Draw or write to explain.

   _____

Solve. Choose a strategy.

· Draw a picture.
· Write a number sentence.

3. Wayne earned a nickel for feeding the cat. He earned a dime for walking the dog. How much money did he earn in all?

   Draw or write to explain.

   _____ cents

Name _____   Date _____

Quarters

Write how many of each coin you need to make 30¢.

1.	1	0	1	0
2.				
3.				
4.				
5.				
6.				

Problem Solving • Reasoning

7. I have 25¢.

Draw 25¢ with fewer coins than I have.	Draw 25¢ with more coins than I have.

Name _____   **Date** _____

Count With Quarters

Circle the coins that match each price.

1.

2.

3.

4.

Problem Solving • Reasoning

5. I count my coins like this: 25¢, 35¢, 45¢, 50¢, 51¢, 52¢, 53¢, 54¢. How many of each coin do I have?

_____ quarters   _____ dimes   _____ nickels   _____ pennies

Name _____ Date _____

Problem Solving:
Use Data From a Picture

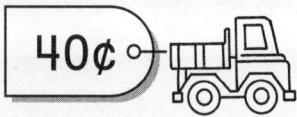

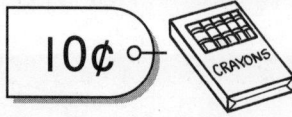

40¢ ○— [toy truck]   10¢ ○— [CRAYONS]   30¢ ○— [Coloring Book]

Solve. Use coins if you want.

1. Jamey wants to buy a toy truck. He has two dimes. How many more dimes does he need?

   Think: Can you count by tens?

   Draw or write to explain.

   _____ dimes

2. Nancy wants to buy crayons. Each box is 10¢. She has 8 nickels. How many boxes of crayons can she buy?

   Think: Can you count by fives?

   Draw or write to explain.

   _____ boxes of crayons

Solve. Choose a strategy.

   • Use models to act it out.
   • Draw a picture.
   • Write a number sentence.

3. Jared has 3 coins. It is enough money to buy a coloring book. What 3 coins does he have?

   Draw or write to explain.

   3 _____

Name _____ **Date** _____

Position Words

Draw each object.

1. ✏ to the right of the ⬭   2. ☕ above the ⬭

3. 🥄 to the left of the ⬭   4. 📏 below the ⬭

5. Circle what is between the 🥄 and ✏.

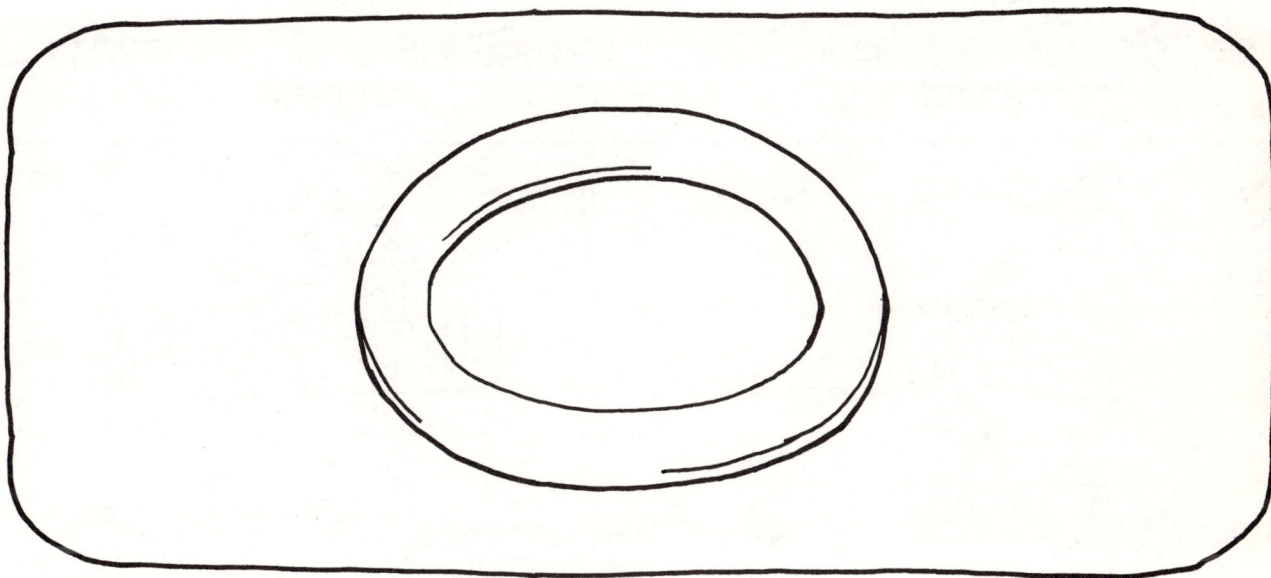

Problem Solving • Reasoning

6. Use the clues to label
   each mouse.
   R is to the left of X.
   C is between X and T.

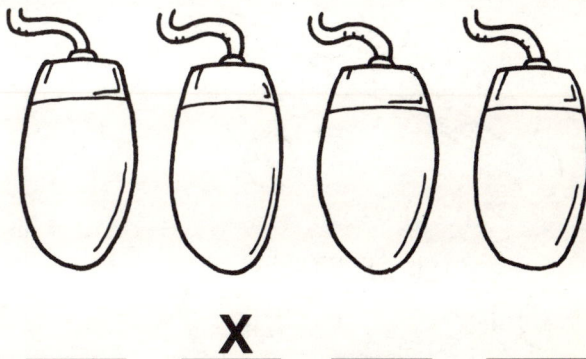

   ___ __X__ ___ ___

Name _____   **Date** _____

More Position Words

Circle the correct words.

1.

The ✋ is next to / behind the 🍎 .

2.

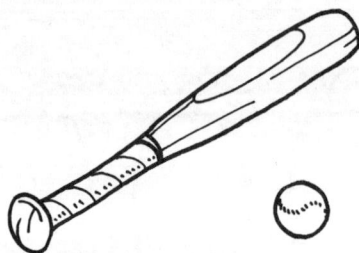

The ✈ is far from / near the ⛰ .

3.

The 🐱 goes up / down the 🌳 .

4.

The ▥ is in front of / behind the 🏠 .

5.

The ⚾ is far from / near the 🏏 .

6.

The 🐌 is far from / near the 🪨 .

Name _____ Date _____

Plane Shapes

Use at least one of each shape to draw a house.

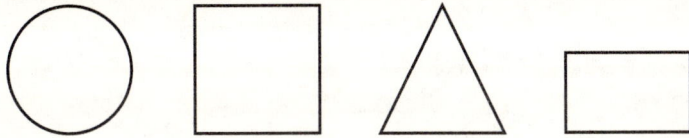

○ □ △ ▭

1. Color circles yellow.

2. Color rectangles blue.

3. Color triangles red.

4. Color squares green.

Problem Solving • Reasoning

5. Circle the puzzle piece that fits.

6. Cut apart one plane shape to make 2 or more puzzle pieces.

Name _____   Date _____

Sorting Shapes

Circle all the shapes that belong in each group.

1. Shapes with 4 corners

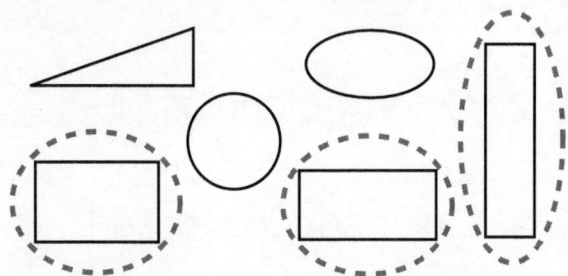

2. Triangles

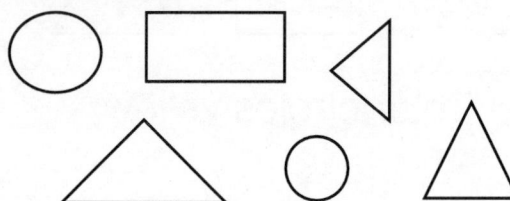

3. Shapes with no corners

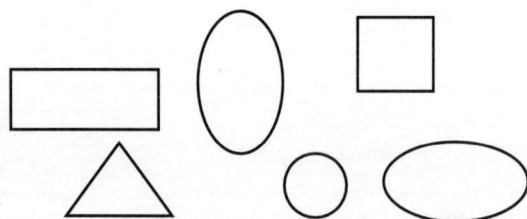

4. Shapes with more than 3 corners

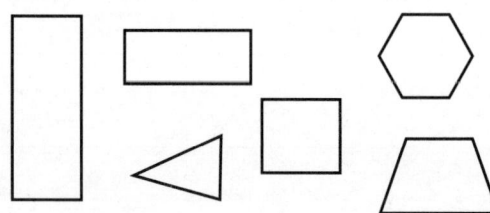

Problem Solving • Reasoning

5. Match each name to the correct shape.

square   triangle   circle   rectangle

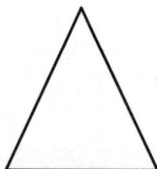      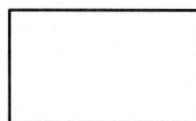   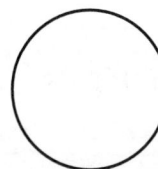

Name _____ **Date** _____

Solid Shapes

Circle objects that have the same shapes.

1.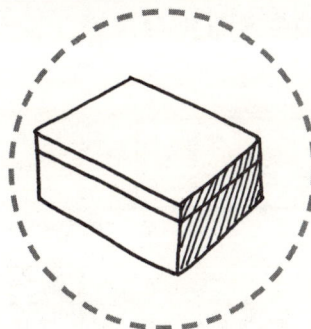

2.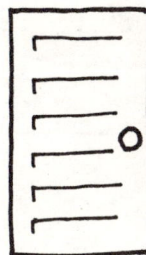

3.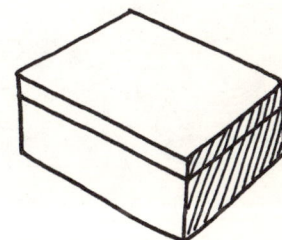

Problem Solving • Reasoning

4. Sort the shapes into two groups. Color one group orange and the other group green. Explain your sorting rule.

 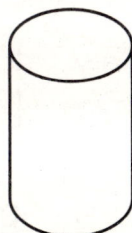 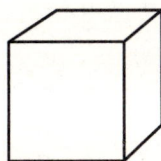 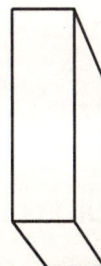 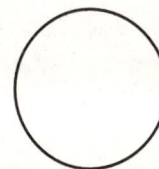

Name _____   Date _____

Identify Faces of a Solid Shape

Circle the object with a face that
matches the plane shape.

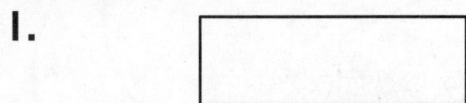

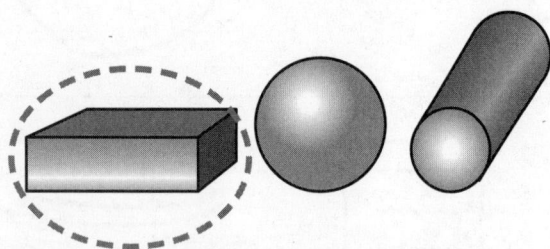

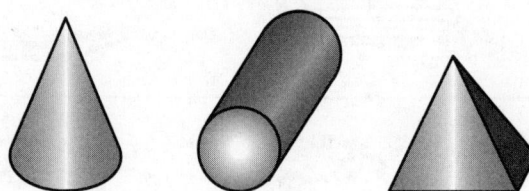

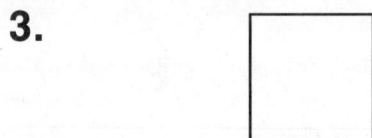

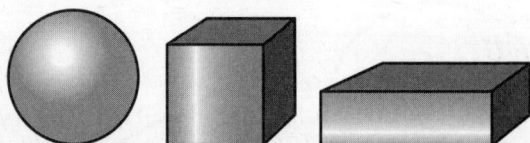

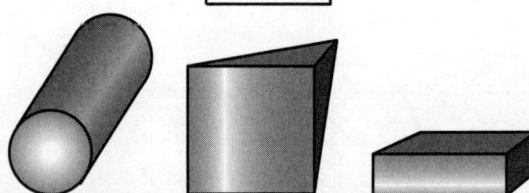

1.

2.

3.

4.

Problem Solving • Reasoning

5. Think about the plane shapes you can see on each
   solid. Make a rule to sort them into two groups.
   Color one group red and the other blue.

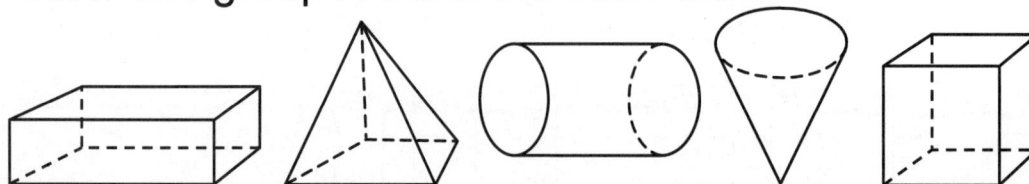

6. **Write About It** Explain how you sorted your groups.

Name _____ **Date** _____

Problem Solving: Find a Pattern

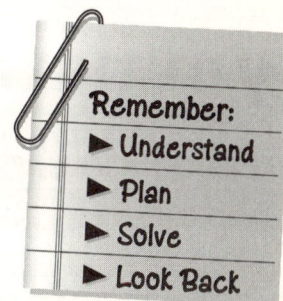

You can use a pattern to solve a problem. Circle the picture that most likely comes next in the pattern.

1. Talia saw this pattern on a pillow case.

Think: Does the cloud or the sun come next?

2. Rose saw this pattern on a book cover.

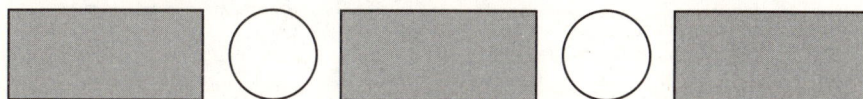

Think: Does the rectangle or the circle come next?

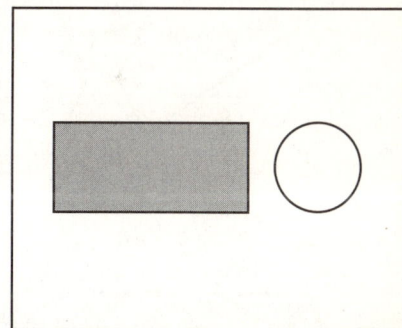

Solve. Choose a strategy.

• Draw a picture.
• Write a number sentence.

3. Eric has 4 stickers on his notebook. Ann has 4 more stickers than Eric. How many stickers does Ann have?

Draw or write to explain.

_____ stickers

Name _____   Date _____

Symmetry

Circle all the shapes that show two matching parts.

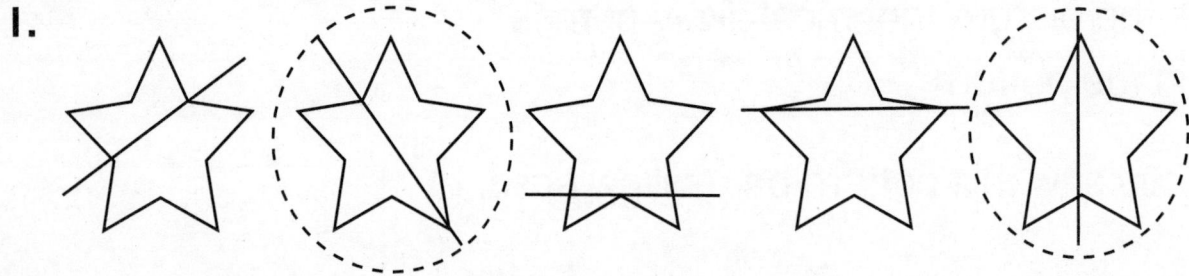

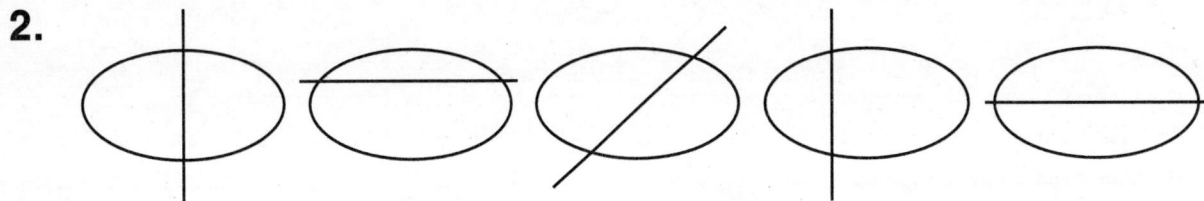

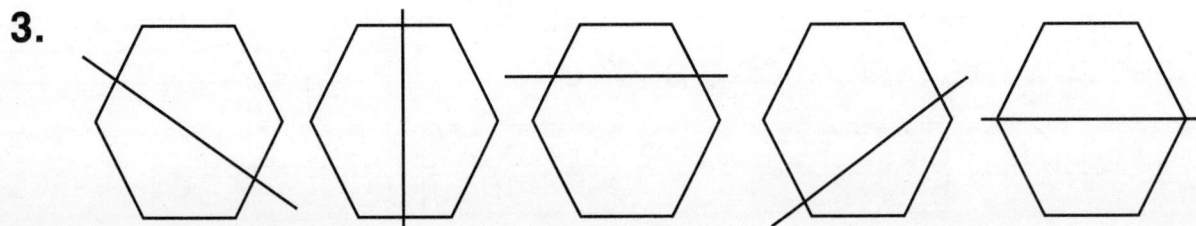

1.

2.

3.

Problem Solving • Reasoning

4. Draw the matching part for each.

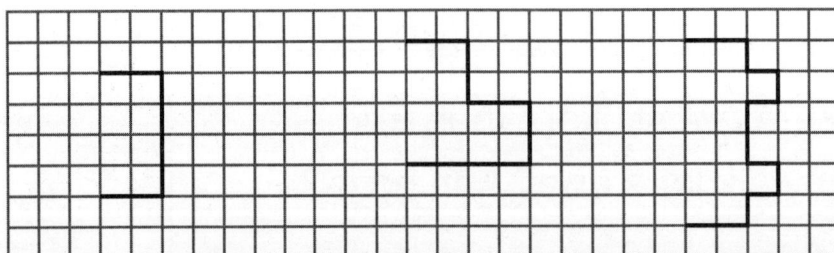

Name _____ Date _____

Equal Parts

Write how many equal parts.

1.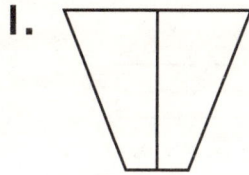

_2_ equal parts

2.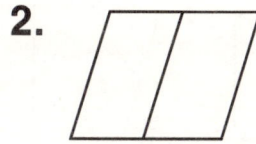

____ equal parts

3.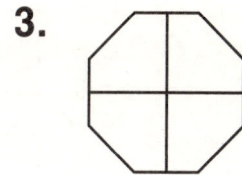

____ equal parts

4.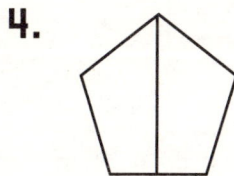

____ equal parts

5.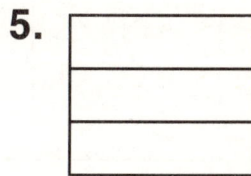

____ equal parts

6.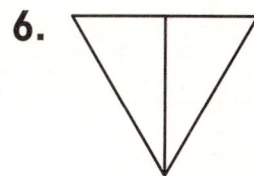

____ equal parts

7.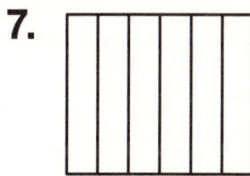

____ equal parts

8.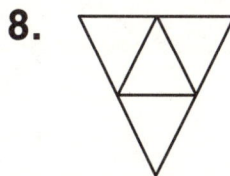

____ equal parts

9.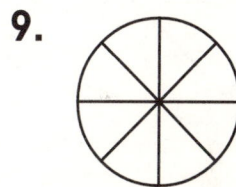

____ equal parts

Problem Solving • Reasoning

10. Draw 4 equal parts in 3 different ways.

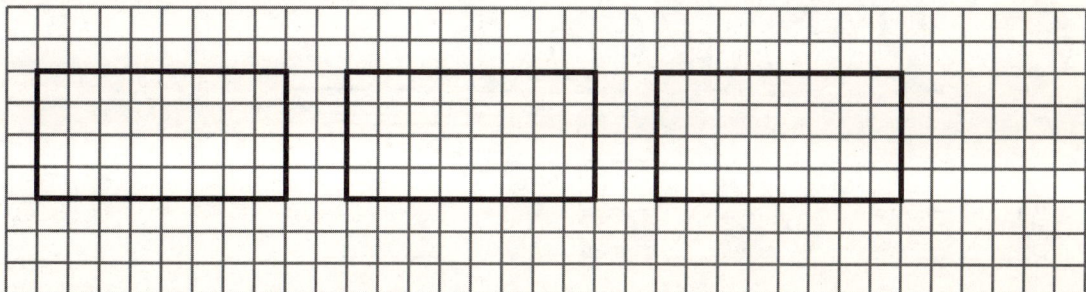

Name _____   Date _____

One Half

Color $\frac{1}{2}$ of each shape.

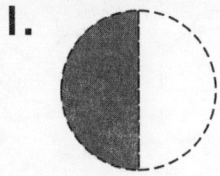

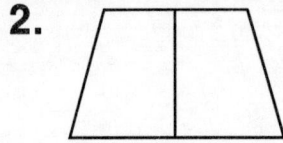

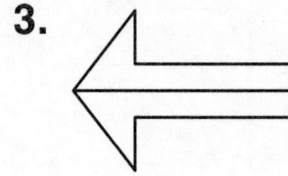

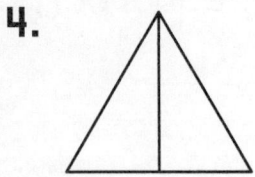

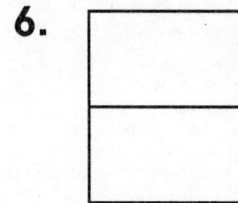

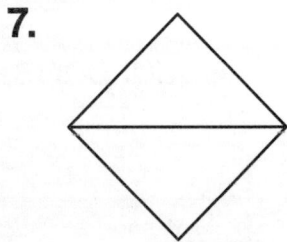

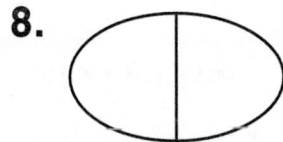

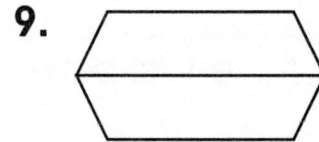

1.

2.

3.

4.

5.

6.

7.

8.

9.

Problem Solving • Reasoning

Draw the shape that is most likely to come next.

10. _____

11. _____

Name _____   **Date** _____

One Third and One Fourth

Color 1 part. Circle each fraction.

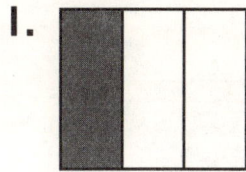

1.

$$\frac{1}{2} \quad \left(\frac{1}{3}\right) \quad \frac{1}{4}$$

2.

$$\frac{1}{2} \quad \frac{1}{3} \quad \frac{1}{4}$$

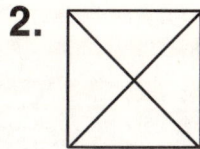

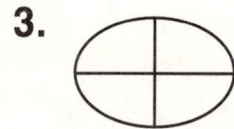

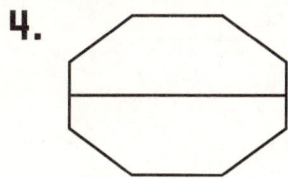

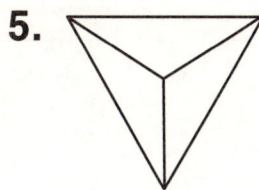

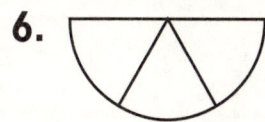

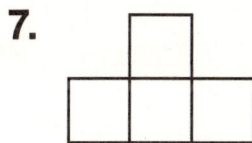

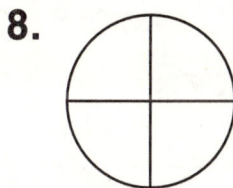

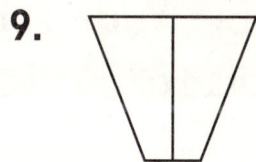

3.

$$\frac{1}{2} \quad \frac{1}{3} \quad \frac{1}{4}$$

4.

$$\frac{1}{2} \quad \frac{1}{3} \quad \frac{1}{4}$$

5.

$$\frac{1}{2} \quad \frac{1}{3} \quad \frac{1}{4}$$

6.

$$\frac{1}{2} \quad \frac{1}{3} \quad \frac{1}{4}$$

7.

$$\frac{1}{2} \quad \frac{1}{3} \quad \frac{1}{4}$$

8.

$$\frac{1}{2} \quad \frac{1}{3} \quad \frac{1}{4}$$

9.

$$\frac{1}{2} \quad \frac{1}{3} \quad \frac{1}{4}$$

Problem Solving • Reasoning

10. Color each to show $\frac{1}{2}$ full.

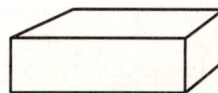

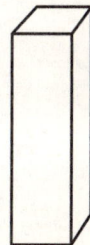

Name _____ Date _____

Spinners and Probability

Use a paper clip and pencil.
Spin 10 times. Record.

1.

Spinner A

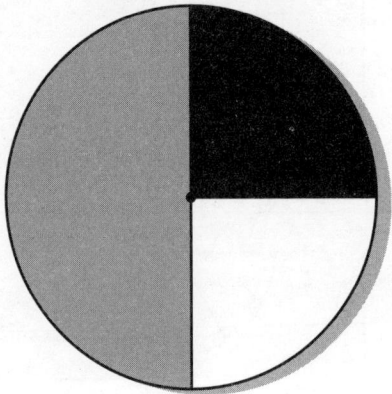

Spinner A		
Color	**Tally**	**Total**
Gray		
White		
Black		

2. Predict which color the spinner will land on
most often. _____

3. Explain Your Thinking Which colors have
an equal chance of being landed on? Why?

_____

Problem Solving • Reasoning

4. Roger has these coins.

Does he have enough money to buy a toy
that costs 50¢? Explain.

Name _____ **Date** _____

Problem Solving: Use Data From a Picture

You can use a picture to help you solve a problem.
Solve. Use data from the picture.

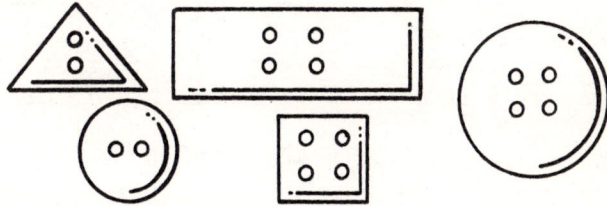

1. How many square buttons are there?

Think: How many equal sides does a square have?

Draw or write to explain.

_____

2. How many buttons have 3 corners?

Think: What shape has 3 corners?

Draw or write to explain.

_____ button

Solve. Choose a strategy.

• Use logical thinking.
• Write a number sentence.

3. Which shape button is shown the most?

Draw or write to explain.

_____

Name _____   Date _____

Add Doubles

Write each sum. Circle the double facts.

1. (⃝ 6 + 6) 12	2. 9 + 9	3. 6 + 3	4. 7 + 7
5. 8 + 1	6. 5 + 5	7. 3 + 4	8. 7 + 2
9. 9 + 3	10. 6 + 5	11. 10 + 10	12. 8 + 8
13. 2 + 9	14. 5 + 7	15. 3 + 8	16. 4 + 4

Problem Solving • Reasoning

17. Ann wants to put these pigs into equal groups. Tell the different ways that she can do this.

Name _____ Date _____

Doubles Plus One

Write each sum. Circle each double fact.
Put a box around each double plus one.

1. $\boxed{\begin{array}{r} 7 \\ +8 \\ \hline 15 \end{array}}$

2. $\begin{array}{r} 9 \\ +9 \\ \hline \end{array}$

3. $\begin{array}{r} 8 \\ +9 \\ \hline \end{array}$

4. $\begin{array}{r} 9 \\ +8 \\ \hline \end{array}$

5. $\begin{array}{r} 7 \\ +6 \\ \hline \end{array}$

6. $\begin{array}{r} 9 \\ +7 \\ \hline \end{array}$

7. $\begin{array}{r} 8 \\ +7 \\ \hline \end{array}$

8. $\begin{array}{r} 4 \\ +5 \\ \hline \end{array}$

9. $\begin{array}{r} 6 \\ +6 \\ \hline \end{array}$

10. $\begin{array}{r} 6 \\ +3 \\ \hline \end{array}$

11. $\begin{array}{r} 4 \\ +4 \\ \hline \end{array}$

12. $\begin{array}{r} 5 \\ +7 \\ \hline \end{array}$

13. $3 + 4 =$ _____

14. $6 + 5 =$ _____

15. $4 + 3 =$ _____

16. $8 + 8 =$ _____

17. $6 + 7 =$ _____

18. $5 + 4 =$ _____

Problem Solving • Reasoning

19. Tiko has 4 crayons. Mel has 1 more crayon than Tiko. How many crayons do Tiko and Mel have together?

Draw or write to explain.

_____ crayons

Name _____ Date _____

Add With Ten

Use paper clips or counters.

Show each number. Write the number sentence.

1. Show 10. Show 5 more.

$$\underline{10} + \underline{5} = \underline{15}$$

2. Show 10. Show 8 more.

___ + ___ = ___

3. Show 10. Show 3 more.

___ + ___ = ___

4. Show 10. Show 6 more.

___ + ___ = ___

Write the sum.

5.   7
  +10
_____

6.   10
  + 4
_____

7.   10
  + 9
_____

8.   2
  +10
_____

9.   5
  +10
_____

10.   10
  + 1
_____

Problem Solving • Reasoning

Write two related subtraction facts for each.

11. $9 + 3 = 12$

___ − ___ = ___

___ − ___ = ___

12. $7 + 8 = 15$

___ − ___ = ___

___ − ___ = ___

Name _____ **Date** _____

Make a Ten to Add

Use paper clips as counters if you want.
Show the numbers. Then add.

1. Show 8 and 5 more.

  _8_ + _5_ = _13_

2. Show 9 and 4 more.

  ___ + ___ = ___

3. Show 7 and 5 more.

  ___ + ___ = ___

4. Show 9 and 8 more.

  ___ + ___ = ___

Add. Use paper clips as counters if you want.

5. 5 +9   6. 8 +7   7. 2 +9   8. 9 +4   9. 7 +5   10. 6 +8

Problem Solving • Reasoning

11. Tom scored 8 points. Then he scored 4 more. How many points does he have now?

Draw or write to explain.

_____ points

Name _____   Date _____

Add Three Numbers

Add.

1.	2.	3.	4.	5.	6.
$\begin{array}{r}4\\6\\+9\\\hline 19\end{array}$	$\begin{array}{r}5\\2\\+5\\\hline\end{array}$	$\begin{array}{r}2\\6\\+8\\\hline\end{array}$	$\begin{array}{r}7\\5\\+3\\\hline\end{array}$	$\begin{array}{r}9\\1\\+3\\\hline\end{array}$	$\begin{array}{r}4\\2\\+8\\\hline\end{array}$

7. $5 + 9 + 3 =$ _____   8. $7 + 0 + 5 =$ _____

9. $2 + 8 + 3 =$ _____   10. $5 + 9 + 4 =$ _____

Problem Solving • Reasoning

11. In the first half of the game, Bo scored 7 points. How many points did Bo score in the game?

    _____ points for Bo

12. Tim scored 4 points in the first half. How many points did Tim score in the game?

    _____ points for Tim

Points Scored in Second Half

Name _____   Date _____

Use Doubles to Subract

Add. Then subtract.

1. $8 + 8 =$ __16__
    $16 - 8 =$ __8__

2. $10 + 10 =$ ____
    $20 - 10 =$ ____

3. $6 + 6 =$ ____
    $12 - 6 =$ ____

4. $9 + 9 =$ ____
    $18 - 9 =$ ____

5. $1 + 1 =$ ____
    $2 - 1 =$ ____

6. $5 + 5 =$ ____
    $10 - 5 =$ ____

7. $\begin{array}{r} 7 \\ +7 \\ \hline \end{array}$ $\begin{array}{r} 14 \\ -\ 7 \\ \hline \end{array}$

8. $\begin{array}{r} 3 \\ +3 \\ \hline \end{array}$ $\begin{array}{r} 6 \\ -3 \\ \hline \end{array}$

9. $\begin{array}{r} 4 \\ +4 \\ \hline \end{array}$ $\begin{array}{r} 8 \\ -4 \\ \hline \end{array}$

10. $\begin{array}{r} 6 \\ +6 \\ \hline \end{array}$ $\begin{array}{r} 12 \\ -\ 6 \\ \hline \end{array}$

11. $\begin{array}{r} 2 \\ +2 \\ \hline \end{array}$ $\begin{array}{r} 4 \\ -2 \\ \hline \end{array}$

12. $\begin{array}{r} 8 \\ +8 \\ \hline \end{array}$ $\begin{array}{r} 16 \\ -\ 8 \\ \hline \end{array}$

Problem Solving • Reasoning

13. Lily has these coins.
    What other coins does she
    need to have 29¢?

    _____

Name _____ Date _____

Subtract From 13 and 14

Add. Then write each difference.

1.
$$
\begin{array}{ccc}
8 & 13 & 13 \\
+5 & -5 & -8 \\
\hline
13 & 8 & 5
\end{array}
$$

2.
$$
\begin{array}{ccc}
10 & 14 & 14 \\
+4 & -4 & -10 \\
\hline
\end{array}
$$

3.
$$
\begin{array}{ccc}
9 & 12 & 12 \\
+3 & -3 & -9 \\
\hline
\end{array}
$$

4.
$$
\begin{array}{ccc}
9 & 14 & 14 \\
+5 & -5 & -9 \\
\hline
\end{array}
$$

5.
$$
\begin{array}{ccc}
8 & 14 & 14 \\
+6 & -6 & -8 \\
\hline
\end{array}
$$

6.
$$
\begin{array}{ccc}
10 & 13 & 13 \\
+3 & -3 & -10 \\
\hline
\end{array}
$$

7.
$$
\begin{array}{ccc}
7 & 13 & 13 \\
+6 & -6 & -7 \\
\hline
\end{array}
$$

8.
$$
\begin{array}{ccc}
4 & 13 & 13 \\
+9 & -9 & -4 \\
\hline
\end{array}
$$

Problem Solving • Reasoning

9. Write an addition sentence to match the picture. Write 2 subtraction sentences.

☆☆☆☆☆☆☆☆
☆☆☆☆☆☆☆

_____ + _____ = _____

_____ − _____ = _____

_____ − _____ = _____

Name _____   Date _____

Subtract From 15 and 16

Add. Then subtract.

1.
```
   8      14      14
 + 6    - 6    - 8
 ‾‾‾‾   ‾‾‾‾   ‾‾‾‾
  14      8      6
```

2.
```
   9      15      15
 + 6    - 6    - 9
 ‾‾‾‾   ‾‾‾‾   ‾‾‾‾
```

3.
```
   7      13      13
 + 6    - 6    - 7
 ‾‾‾‾   ‾‾‾‾   ‾‾‾‾
```

4.
```
   8      15      15
 + 7    - 7    - 8
 ‾‾‾‾   ‾‾‾‾   ‾‾‾‾
```

5.
```
  10      15      15
 + 5    - 5    -10
 ‾‾‾‾   ‾‾‾‾   ‾‾‾‾
```

6.
```
   4      13      13
 + 9    - 9    - 4
 ‾‾‾‾   ‾‾‾‾   ‾‾‾‾
```

7.
```
   6      16      16
 +10    -10    - 6
 ‾‾‾‾   ‾‾‾‾   ‾‾‾‾
```

8.
```
   7      16      16
 + 9    - 7    - 9
 ‾‾‾‾   ‾‾‾‾   ‾‾‾‾
```

Problem Solving • Reasoning

9. Write the word name for the number that completes the sentence.

Sixteen minus five equals _____.

Fifteen minus twelve equals _____.

Name _____   Date _____

Subtract From 17 Through 20

Subtract.

1.	2.	3.	4.	5.	6.
18 − 9 **9**	15 − 7	19 −10	16 − 9	14 − 5	20 −10

7.	8.	9.	10.	11.	12.
13 − 5	15 − 9	18 −10	17 − 8	16 − 8	17 −10

13.	14.	15.	16.	17.	18.
19 − 9	17 − 9	18 − 8	15 − 5	14 − 5	15 − 5

Write a subtraction sentence. Then write the difference.

19. Pam has 19 golf balls. She gave 9 balls to Ted. How many golf balls does Pam have now?

____ − ____ = ____

_____ golf balls

20. Ed has 17 golf tees. He gave 9 tees to Rick. How many golf tees does Ed have now?

____ − ____ = ____

_____ golf tees

Name _____ Date _____

Problem Solving: Write a Number Sentence

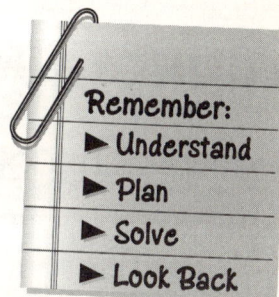

Remember:
► Understand
► Plan
► Solve
► Look Back

You can write a number sentence to help you solve problems.

Solve. Write a number sentence.

1. Tyler catches 8 fish on a fishing trip. Sarah catches 5 fish. How many more fish did Tyler catch than Sarah?

Think: How can I find out how many more?

Draw or write to explain.

_____ ◯ _____ = _____ fish

2. Tamara's team scored 9 goals on Friday, 7 goals on Saturday, and 3 goals on Sunday. How many goals did they score in all?

Think: What do I need to find out?

Draw or write to explain.

_____ ◯ _____ ◯ _____ = _____ goals

Solve. Choose a strategy.

• Write a number sentence.
• Draw a picture.

3. Daniel paints 15 pictures. 7 of them have animals in them. How many pictures do not have animals in them?

Draw or write to explain.

_____ ◯ _____ = _____ pictures

Name _____   Date _____

Algebra Readiness: Fact Families

Write each fact family.

1.

16	
7	9

$$7 \; \substack{+} \; 9 = 16$$

$$9 \; \substack{+} \; 7 = 16$$

$$16 \; \substack{-} \; 9 = 7$$

$$16 \; \substack{-} \; 7 = 9$$

2.

14	
6	8

3.

15	
7	8

Problem Solving • Reasoning

4. Use the code.

Complete each number sentence.

Code

★ = 7   ▼ = 5

★ + ▼ = ____   ▼ + ▼ = ____

Name _____   **Date** _____

Algebra Readiness:
Relate Addition and Subtraction

Write the missing numbers.

1. $20 - 10 = \underline{10}$

   $20 = 10 + \underline{10}$

2. $11 - 6 = \underline{\hspace{1cm}}$

   $11 = 6 + \underline{\hspace{1cm}}$

3. $15 - 7 = \underline{\hspace{1cm}}$

   $15 = 7 + \underline{\hspace{1cm}}$

4. $13 - 8 = \underline{\hspace{1cm}}$

   $13 = 8 + \underline{\hspace{1cm}}$

5. $14 - 7 = \underline{\hspace{1cm}}$

   $14 = 7 + \underline{\hspace{1cm}}$

6. $12 - 7 = \underline{\hspace{1cm}}$

   $12 = 7 + \underline{\hspace{1cm}}$

7. $19 - 10 = \underline{\hspace{1cm}}$

   $19 = 10 + \underline{\hspace{1cm}}$

8. $15 - 9 = \underline{\hspace{1cm}}$

   $15 = 9 + \underline{\hspace{1cm}}$

9. $16 - 8 = \underline{\hspace{1cm}}$

   $16 = 8 + \underline{\hspace{1cm}}$

Problem Solving • Reasoning

10. Write a fact family by using the numbers outside the circle but inside the square.

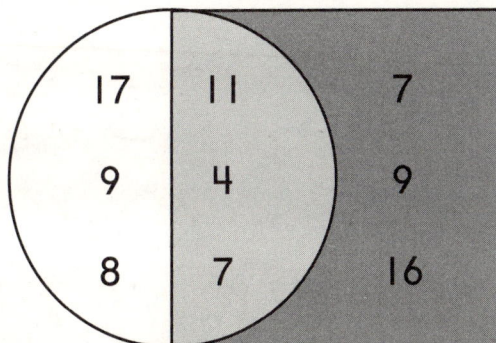

$\underline{\hspace{1cm}} + \underline{\hspace{1cm}} = \underline{\hspace{1cm}}$

$\underline{\hspace{1cm}} + \underline{\hspace{1cm}} = \underline{\hspace{1cm}}$

$\underline{\hspace{1cm}} - \underline{\hspace{1cm}} = \underline{\hspace{1cm}}$

$\underline{\hspace{1cm}} - \underline{\hspace{1cm}} = \underline{\hspace{1cm}}$

17	11	7
9	4	9
8	7	16

Use with text pages 427–428.   **113**

Name _____   **Date** _____

Different Ways to Subtract

Write each difference.

1. 16
  − 8
  8

2. 13
  − 7

3. 20
  −10

4. 18
  −10

5. 14
  − 6

6. 19
  − 9

7. 12
  − 6

8. 12
  − 5

9. 15
  − 8

10. 13
  − 9

11. 18
  − 8

12. 14
  − 8

13. 17
  − 7

14. 13
  − 5

15. 16
  − 9

16. 14
  − 7

17. 17
  − 9

18. 15
  − 5

19. 17
  −10

20. 19
  −10

Problem Solving • Reasoning

21. Half the caps are Sid's.
    Half the caps are Jay's.
    How many are
    Sid's? _____
    Tell how you know.

Name _____   Date _____

Problem Solving: Choose the Operation

Write the number sentence.
Add or subtract to solve.

1. Manny places 8 stickers in his scrapbook. He then places 6 more. How many stickers did he put in his scrapbook in all?

Think:
What do I need to find out?

Draw or write to explain.

_____ stickers

2. Theresa takes 15 pictures. 6 of them are at the circus. How many pictures were not at the circus?

Think:
What do I already know?

Draw or write to explain.

_____ pictures

Solve. Choose a strategy.

· Use models to act it out.
· Write a number sentence.

3. There are 20 lines on a page in Sarah's journal. She writes on 10 lines. How many lines are left?

Draw or write to explain.

_____ lines

Name _____ Date _____

Compare Length and Height

Circle the tallest. Put a box around the shortest.

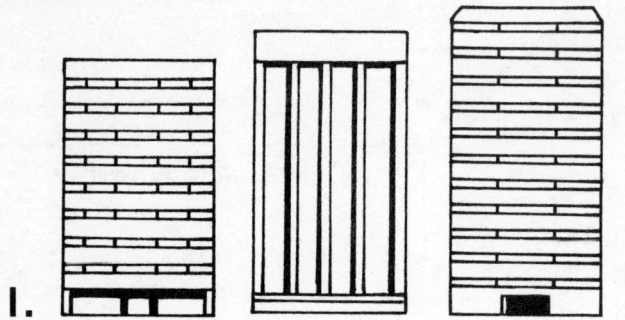

1.

2.

Circle the longest. Put a box around the shortest.

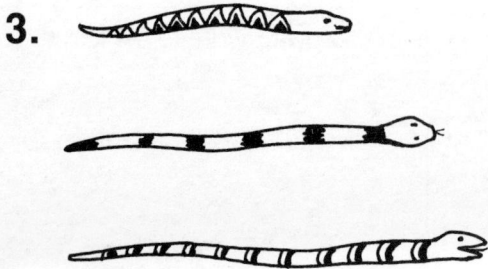

3.

4.

Problem Solving • Reasoning

5. Use the clues to draw the picture. The tree is the tallest. The house is taller than Lori. The flowers are shorter than Lori.

| Draw or write to explain. |

Name _____ Date _____

Nonstandard Units

Estimate. Measure with a ⬭═══ .

	Find the object.	Estimate.	Measure.
1.		about _____ ⬭═══	_____ ⬭═══
2.		about _____ ⬭═══	_____ ⬭═══
3.		about _____ ⬭═══	_____ ⬭═══
4.		about _____ ⬭═══	_____ ⬭═══

Problem Solving • Reasoning

5. Circle the objects that cannot roll.

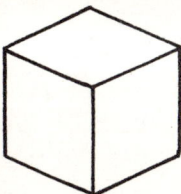

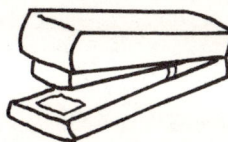

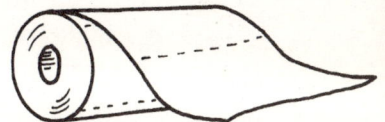

Name _____   Date _____

Inches

Use an inch ruler.

1. Measure each part to the nearest inch.

_____ inch   _____ inch   _____ inches   _____ inches   _____ inch

Problem Solving • Reasoning

2. Use an inch ruler to draw a line that is 3 inches long in the space below.

Name _____ **Date** _____

Centimeters

Use a centimeter ruler. Measure each object.
Remember to line up your ruler on the left.

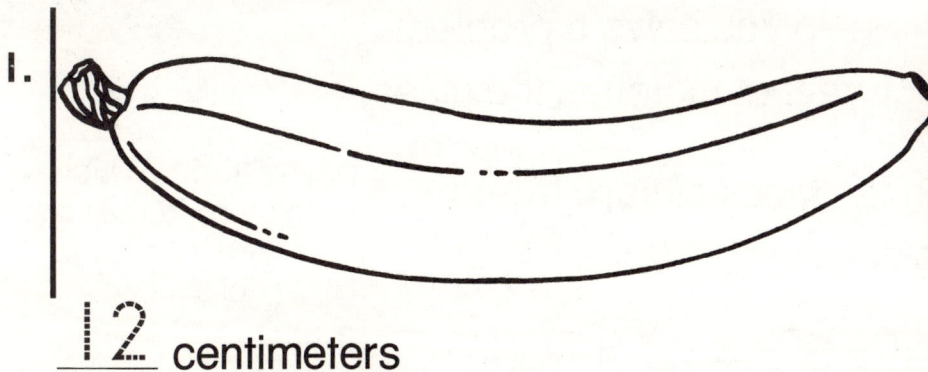

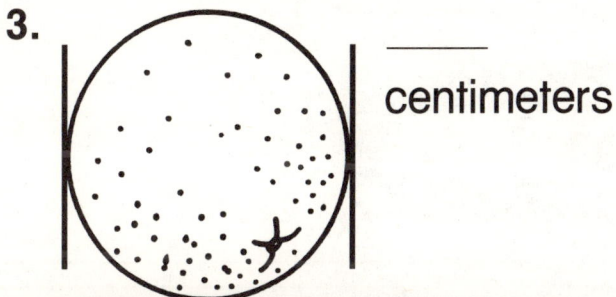

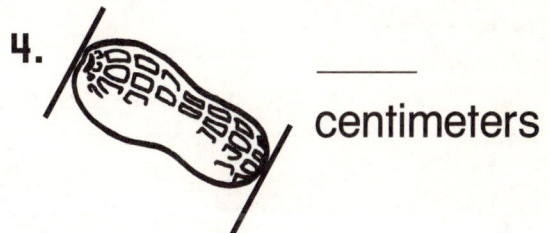

1. _12_ centimeters

2. _____ centimeters

3. _____ centimeters

4. _____ centimeters

Problem Solving • Reasoning

5. Color the longest pencil.

6. Put an X on the shortest pencil.

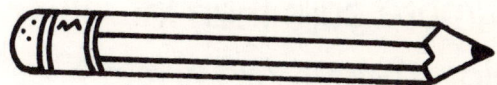

7. Circle the pencil that is about 6 centimeters long.

Name _____   Date _____

Problem Solving: Logical Thinking

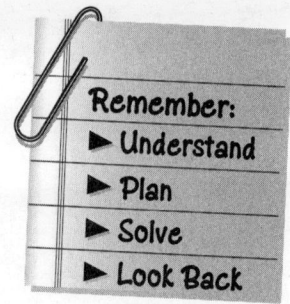

Remember:
► Understand
► Plan
► Solve
► Look Back

You can use clues to help you solve a problem.

Solve. Circle the picture that matches the clues.

1. It is bigger than the black picture frame.
   It has a star on it.

   Think: Which picture frames are larger than the black one?

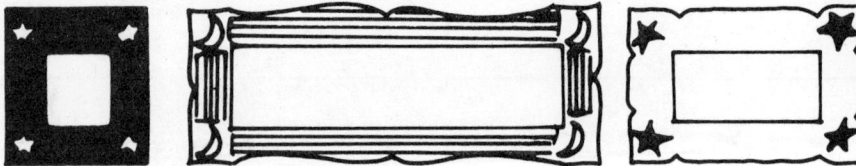

2. It has a sun on it.
   It is not white.

   Think: Which ones have a sun on them?

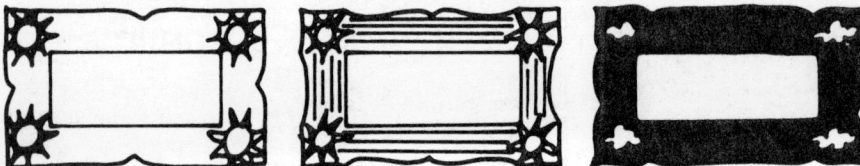

Solve. Choose a strategy.

- Use models to act it out.
- Write a number sentence.

3. Herb has 13 toy cars. He keeps the cars in two cases. One case has 3 more cars than the other case has. How many cars are in each case?

   Draw or write to explain.

   _____ cars   _____ cars

Name _____   Date _____

Compare Weight

Circle the heavier one in each.

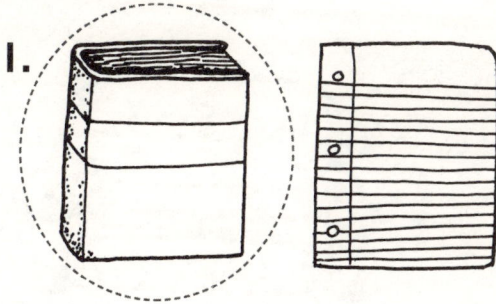

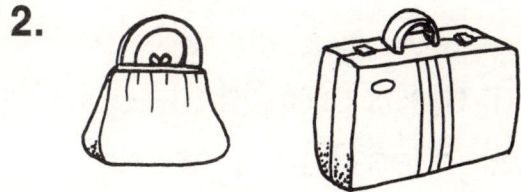

1.

2.

Circle the lighter one in each.

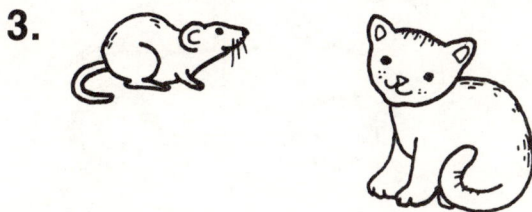

3.

4.

Problem Solving • Reasoning

Logical Thinking

5. Use the clues to label the dolls.
   Marie is heavier than Rose. Rose
   is heavier than Laura.

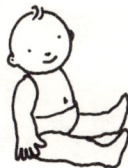

_____   _____   _____

Name _____ Date _____

Pounds

1. Circle the objects that weigh more than
   1 pound.

2. Put a box around the objects that
   weigh less that 1 pound.

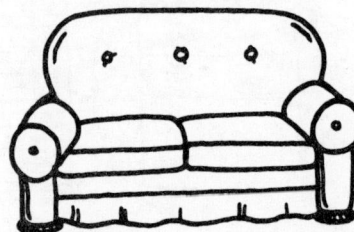

Problem Solving • Reasoning

3. Anna has these coins. She buys
   a post card for 36¢. How much
   money does she have left?

   _____ ¢

4. Explain what coins Anna might
   have left.

Name _____ **Date** _____

Kilograms

1. Circle the objects that are more than 1 kilogram.

2. Put a box around the objects that are less than 1 kilogram.

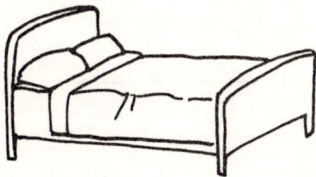

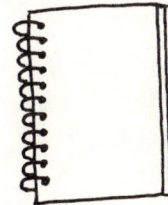

Problem Solving • Reasoning

3. Write 1, 10, or 100 under the correct picture.

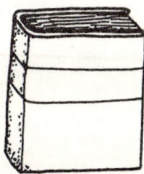

about _____ kilogram

about _____ kilograms

about _____ kilograms

Name _____ **Date** _____

Compare Capacity

Number the containers in order from the least to
the greatest amount held.

1.

2 3 1

2.

___   ___   ___

3.

___   ___   ___

Problem Solving • Reasoning

4. Circle the best jar to hold the pencils.

Name _____ **Date** _____

Cups, Pints, and Quarts

You can use cups, pints, and quarts to tell how much a container holds.

Circle the ones that hold the same amount.

1.

2.

3.

Problem Solving • Reasoning

4. The pot holds _____ more cups than the bottle.

5. **Write Your Own**
   Write a question you can answer by using the graph.

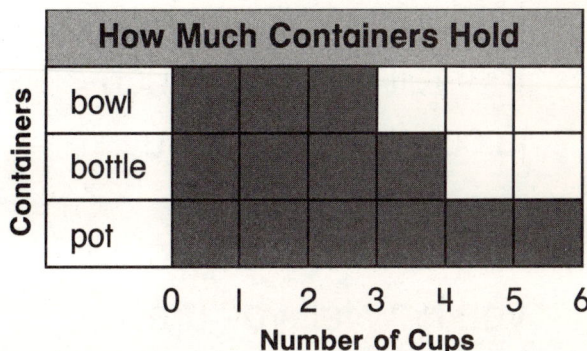

How Much Containers Hold

Containers						
bowl						
bottle						
pot						

0 1 2 3 4 5 6
Number of Cups

Name _____ Date _____

Liters

1. Circle the containers that hold more than 1 liter.

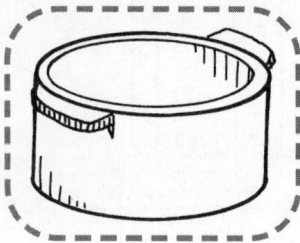

I liter

Problem Solving • Reasoning

2. Underline the words that tell you how much juice you drank today.

cup   liter

centimeter   quart

3. Circle the words that tell you how tall you are.

pint   inch

Name _____ **Date** _____

Problem Solving:
Use Measurement

Use measurement to solve each problem.

1. Howard has a large paper clip that is 5 centimeters long. Jane has a small paper clip that is 3 centimeters long. How much longer is Howard's paper clip than Becky's paper clip?

Think: Do I add or subtract?

Draw or write to explain.

_____ centimeters

2. Ira wants to make lemonade. What should he use to measure the water?

Think: Do I use a cup or a ruler?

Draw or write to explain.

_____

Solve. Choose a strategy.

• Write a number sentence.
• Draw a picture.

3. Archie helps Ira make the lemonade. He measures 4 cups of water into the pitcher. How many pints is this?

Draw or write to explain.

_____ pints

Name _____ Date _____

Order Events

Write **1**, **2**, and **3** to show the correct order.

1.

1   3   2

2.

Problem Solving • Reasoning

Eve went to school today. Next, she played a game. Then she had a snack.

3. What did Eve do before she
played a game? _____

4. What did Eve do after she
played a game? _____

Name _____ Date _____

Compare Time

Circle the activity that takes a shorter time to do.

1.

Circle the activity that takes a longer time to do.

2.

Problem Solving • Reasoning

3. Which food took the shortest time to prepare? _____

4. Which food took the longer time to prepare? _____

A

B

C

Name _____   Date _____

Hour

Write each time. **Remember:** The shorter hand is the hour hand.

1.

5 o'clock

2.

_____ o'clock

3.
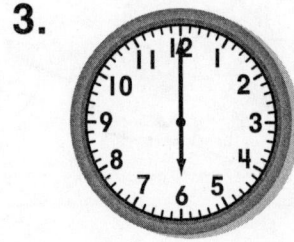
_____ o'clock

4.

_____ o'clock

5.

_____ o'clock

6.

_____ o'clock

Problem Solving • Reasoning

7. How many children have games that start at 3 o'clock?

_____ children

8. How many children have games that start at 4 o'clock?

_____ children

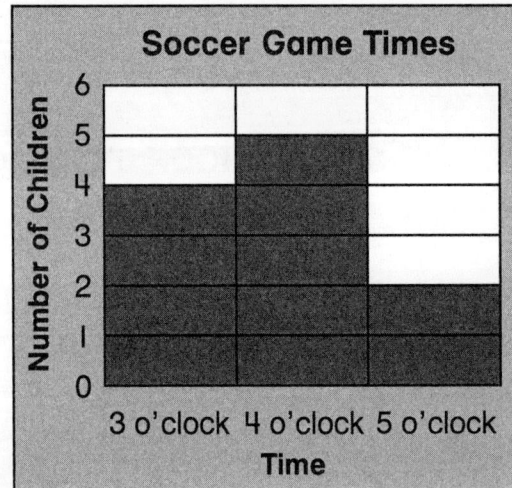
Soccer Game Times

Name _____ Date _____

Half-Hour

Write each time. Think about the number that
the hour hand has moved past.

1.

half past _____

2.

half past _____

3.

half past _____

4.

half past _____

5.

half past _____

6.

half past _____

Problem Solving • Reasoning

Circle the correct words.

7. It takes about _____
to write your name.

   a minute   an hour

8. When it is half-past 3,
the _____ points to 6.

   minute hand   hour hand

Name _____ **Date** _____

Write Time Another Way

Write each time two ways.

1.  2 : 30

half past 2

2.  ___ : ___

_____ o'clock

3.  ___ : ___

_____ o'clock

4.  ___ : ___

half past _____

5.  ___ : ___

_____ o'clock

6.  ___ : ___

half past _____

Problem Solving • Reasoning

7. Write the time each clock shows.

___ : ___   ___ : ___   ___ : ___   ___ : ___

8. Write About It Write about the pattern you see above.

Name _____ **Date** _____

Digital Clocks

Draw lines to match the clocks.

1.

2.

3.

4.

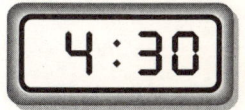

5.

6.

7.

8.

Problem Solving • Reasoning

The clocks show when the children go to school.

Lora   Heather   Abe

9. Who leaves first?   **10.** Who leaves after Heather?

_____   _____

Name _____   Date _____

Practice Telling Time

Show the time on the clock.

1. On Saturday we wake up at 8:30.

2. We feed the dog at 9:00.

3. Art class starts at 1:00.

4. The soccer game is at 2:30.

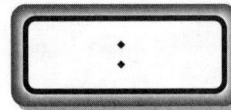

5. We have a snack at 4:00.

6. Dinner is at 6:00.

Problem Solving • Reasoning

7. Fill in the times on the schedule.

Breakfast _____:_____

Lunch _____:_____   Dinner _____:_____

Name _____   **Date** _____

Elapsed Time

Show when each activity started or ended. Use
a clock if you want.

	Start	How long?	Finish
1.	(clock showing 12:00)	$\frac{1}{2}$ hour driving	(clock showing 12:30)
2.	(clock showing 1:00)	I hour having lunch	(clock showing 2:00)
3.	(:)	3 hours walking	5:00

Problem Solving • Reasoning

Write About It

4. Anna has these coins.
   Can she buy a ring
   that costs 40¢?
   Explain.

_____

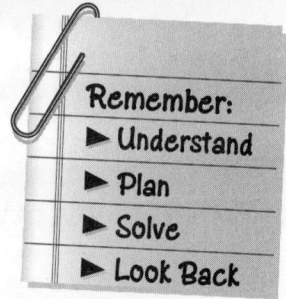

Name _____ Date _____

Problem Solving: Use Models to Act It Out

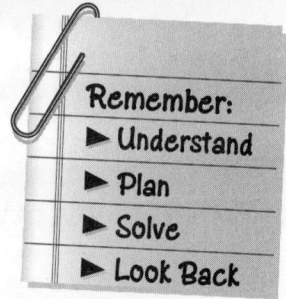

You can use a clock to act out problems with time. Solve. Use a clock if you need to.

1. The pony rides start at 4:00. They will run for 3 hours. What time do they end?

Think: Will the hour hand move 3 hours or 3 half-hours?

Draw or write to explain.

_____

2. The trapeze act starts at 11:00. It ends at 1:00. How long does the trapeze act take?

Think: How many hours are between 11:00 and 1:00?

Draw or write to explain.

_____ hours

Solve. Choose a strategy.

· Use logical thinking.
· Draw a picture.
· Use models to act it out.

3. The Big Top Circus is 3 hours long. It starts at 12:00. What time will it end?

Draw or write to explain.

_____

Name _____   Date _____

Calendar

Fill in the calendar for next month.
Answer the questions.

Sunday	**Monday**	**Tuesday**	**Wednesday**	**Thursday**	**Friday**	**Saturday**

1. Use a red crayon to color the first day of the month.

2. Use a blue crayon to color the first Tuesday of the month.

3. Use the purple crayon to color tomorrow.

4. Use a yellow crayon to color the last day of the month.

5. Put an X on the second Saturday of the month.

6. How many Tuesdays are in this month?

_____

Name _____   Date _____

Use a Calendar

Use the calendars to answer each question.

SEPTEMBER 2002						
Sunday	Monday	Tuesday	Wednesday	Thursday	Friday	Saturday
1	2	3	4	5	6	7
8	9	10	11	12	13	14
15	16	17	18	19	20	21
22	23	24	25	26	27	28
29	30					

OCTOBER 2002						
Sunday	Monday	Tuesday	Wednesday	Thursday	Friday	Saturday
		1	2	3	4	5
6	7	8	9	10	11	12
13	14	15	16	17	18	19
20	21	22	23	24	25	26
27	28	29	30	31		

NOVEMBER 2002						
Sunday	Monday	Tuesday	Wednesday	Thursday	Friday	Saturday
					1	2
3	4	5	6	7	8	9
10	11	12	13	14	15	16
17	18	19	20	21	22	23
24	25	26	27	28	29	30

1. Which month has the most days?

   _____

2. Which month has 5 Fridays?

   _____

3. Color in orange the fifth Thursday in October.

4. Color in red the second Friday in September.

5. November 28 is Thanksgiving. Color it brown.

6. Draw an X on all the Wednesdays in September.

Problem Solving • Reasoning

Find each sum. Then write the addends.

7. _____ + _____ = [   ] ←— 3rd Saturday in October.

8. _____ + _____ = [   ] ←— 3rd Thursday in October.

Name _____ Date _____

Problem Solving: Use a Table

Saturday Schedule	
Sign in	9:00
Baseball game	10:00
Lunch	12:00
Trip to boardwalk	1:00
Dinner	7:00

You can use the information in a table to help you solve problems.

Use the table to solve each problem.

1. What activity begins 6 hours before dinner?

   Think: What time is dinner?

   Draw or write to explain.

   _____

2. How many hours are between the sign in and lunch?

   Think: What time is lunch?

   Draw or write to explain.

   _____ hours

Solve. Choose a strategy.
Use the table if you need to.

• Write a number sentence.
• Use models to act it out.
• Use logical thinking.

3. How many hours are planned for the baseball game?

   Draw or write to explain.

   _____ hours

Name _____   Date _____

Mental Math: Add Tens

Write the numbers. Add.

1.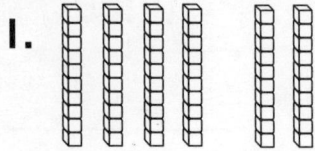

4 tens + 2 tens = __6__ tens

__40__ + __20__ = __60__

2.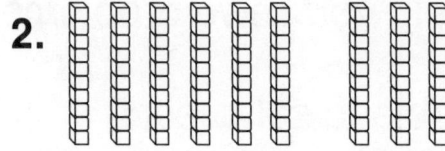

6 tens + 3 tens = _____ tens

_____ + _____ = _____

---

3. 3 tens + 1 ten = _____ tens

_____ + _____ = _____

4. 2 tens + 6 tens = _____ tens

_____ + _____ = _____

---

5. 2 tens + 3 tens = _____ tens

_____ + _____ = _____

6. 1 ten + 1 ten = _____ tens

_____ + _____ = _____

---

7. 1 ten + 7 tens = _____ tens

_____ + _____ = _____

8. 4 tens + 4 tens = _____ tens

_____ + _____ = _____

Problem Solving • Reasoning

9. Jeanne has 40 crayons. Her aunt gives her some more. Now she has 90 crayons. How many crayons did her aunt give her?

_____ crayons

Draw or write to explain.

Name _____ Date _____

Add One-Digit Numbers

Use a workmat with ▭ and ▫ .
Write each sum.

1.
Tens	Ones
2	4
+	3
2	7

2.
Tens	Ones
7	8
+	1

3.
Tens	Ones
5	1
+	6

4.
Tens	Ones
4	5
+	4

5.
Tens	Ones
3	3
+	5

6.
Tens	Ones
8	2
+	7

7.
Tens	Ones
6	2
+	3

8.
Tens	Ones
9	7
+	1

9.
Tens	Ones
3	1
+	8

10.
Tens	Ones
7	4
+	4

11.
Tens	Ones
6	7
+	2

12.
Tens	Ones
5	2
+	3

Problem Solving • Reasoning

13. Color the shapes used to make this picture.

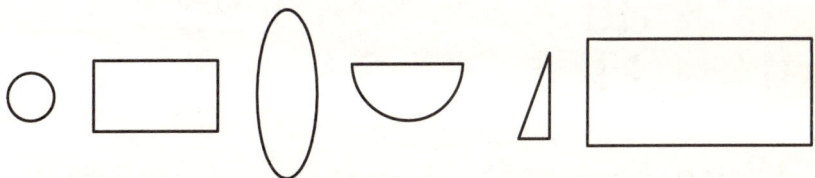

Name _____ Date _____

Add Two-Digit Numbers

Write each sum.

1.
Tens	Ones
3	1
+ 1	4
4	5

2.
Tens	Ones
4	4
+ 3	5

3.
Tens	Ones
5	6
+ 1	3

4.
Tens	Ones
1	3
+ 1	6

5.
Tens	Ones
2	8
+ 3	1

6.
Tens	Ones
7	0
+ 1	8

7.
Tens	Ones
5	2
+ 3	5

8.
Tens	Ones
5	4
+ 4	2

9.
Tens	Ones
1	8
+ 6	1

10.
Tens	Ones
6	5
+ 2	2

11.
Tens	Ones
2	0
+ 7	7

12.
Tens	Ones
2	4
+ 1	1

Problem Solving • Reasoning

Circle the one with the greatest sum.

13. 41 + 25
    41 + 38
    41 + 11

14. 36 + 13
    36 + 23
    36 + 32

15. 57 + 10
    57 + 41
    57 + 32

16. **Write About It** How do you know which sum is greatest?

Name _____ Date _____

Different Ways to Add

Choose a way to add. Write each sum.

1.
Tens	Ones
1	3
+ 2	5
3	8

2.
Tens	Ones
4	2
+ 3	6

3.
Tens	Ones
2	6
+ 2	3

4. 47
   +22

5. 25
   +52

6. 84
   +12

7. 60
   + 9

8. 42
   + 7

9. 16
   + 3

10. 38
    +10

11. 75
    + 0

12. 32
    +16

13. 26
    +51

14. $73 + 5 =$ ____

15. $30 + 60 =$ ____

16. $85 + 4 =$ ____

Problem Solving • Reasoning

17. Laura has 61 marbles in one box. Her best friend gives her 32 marbles in another box. How many marbles does Laura have in all?

Draw or write to explain.

____ marbles

Name _____ Date _____

Practice Two-Digit Addition

Add. Color all sums less than 50.

1. $\begin{array}{r} 17 \\ +50 \\ \hline 67 \end{array}$	**2.** $\begin{array}{r} 65 \\ +24 \\ \hline \end{array}$	**3.** $\begin{array}{r} 44 \\ +12 \\ \hline \end{array}$	**4.** $\begin{array}{r} 33 \\ +34 \\ \hline \end{array}$	**5.** $\begin{array}{r} 24 \\ +21 \\ \hline \end{array}$
6. $\begin{array}{r} 81 \\ +11 \\ \hline \end{array}$	**7.** $\begin{array}{r} 61 \\ +18 \\ \hline \end{array}$	**8.** $\begin{array}{r} 52 \\ +47 \\ \hline \end{array}$	**9.** $\begin{array}{r} 18 \\ +20 \\ \hline \end{array}$	**10.** $\begin{array}{r} 16 \\ +32 \\ \hline \end{array}$
11. $\begin{array}{r} 57 \\ +\ 2 \\ \hline \end{array}$	**12.** $\begin{array}{r} 31 \\ +25 \\ \hline \end{array}$	**13.** $\begin{array}{r} 40 \\ +30 \\ \hline \end{array}$	**14.** $\begin{array}{r} 96 \\ +\ 3 \\ \hline \end{array}$	**15.** $\begin{array}{r} 26 \\ +72 \\ \hline \end{array}$
16. $\begin{array}{r} 49 \\ +20 \\ \hline \end{array}$	**17.** $\begin{array}{r} 37 \\ +22 \\ \hline \end{array}$	**18.** $\begin{array}{r} 21 \\ +16 \\ \hline \end{array}$	**19.** $\begin{array}{r} 36 \\ +13 \\ \hline \end{array}$	**20.** $\begin{array}{r} 18 \\ +11 \\ \hline \end{array}$

21. Marta has 27 baseball cards. Robert gives her 32 more cards. How many does she have in all?

_____ baseball cards

22. Robin sent out 23 invitations to her party. Then she sent out 11 more. How many did she send out in all?

_____ invitations

Name _____   Date _____

Problem Solving: Make a Table

Remember:
- ► Understand
- ► Plan
- ► Solve
- ► Look Back

Sometimes you can make a table to help you solve a problem.

Toys	Number
Books	
Toy Cars	21
Jacks	

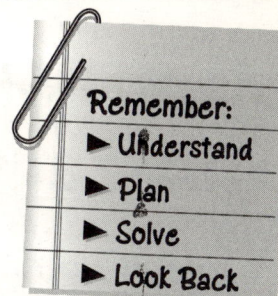

Solve. Use the answers to complete the table.

1. There are 5 more books than toy cars. How many books are there?

   _____ books

   Think: Do I add or subtract?

   Draw or write to explain.

2. There are 12 more jacks than toy cars. How many jacks are there?

   _____ jacks

   Think: What numbers do I use?

   Draw or write to explain.

Choose a strategy. Solve. Use the table.

- • Make a table.
- • Use logical thinking.
- • Write a number sentence.

3. How many jacks and books are there in all?

   _____ jacks and books

   Draw or write to explain.

Name _____ **Date** _____

Mental Math:
Subtract Tens

Write the numbers. Subtract.

1. [tens blocks: 7 groups]

7 tens − 6 tens = __1__ ten

70 − 60 = 10

2. [tens blocks: 4 groups]

4 tens − 1 ten = _____ tens

_____ − _____ = _____

3. 9 tens − 2 tens = _____ tens

_____ − _____ = _____

4. 5 tens − 1 ten = _____ tens

_____ − _____ = _____

5. 8 tens − 6 tens = _____ tens

_____ − _____ = _____

6. 8 tens − 3 tens = _____ tens

_____ − _____ = _____

Problem Solving • Reasoning

Use the bar graph.

7. How many more red flowers than pink flowers does Neal have?

_____ more flowers

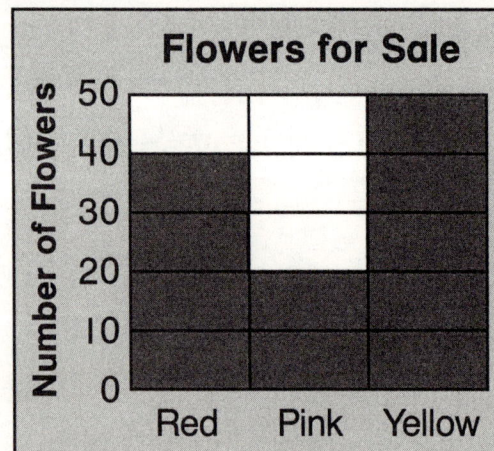

Flowers for Sale

Number of Flowers: 0, 10, 20, 30, 40, 50

Red   Pink   Yellow

Name _____   Date _____

Subtract One-Digit Numbers

Use a workmat with ▭▭▭ and ▢.
Write each difference.

1.
Tens	Ones
6	7
−	3
6	4

2.
Tens	Ones
8	8
−	1

3.
Tens	Ones
4	6
−	5

4.
Tens	Ones
5	9
−	6

5.
Tens	Ones
9	4
−	2

6.
Tens	Ones
2	1
−	1

7.
Tens	Ones
3	8
−	4

8.
Tens	Ones
1	8
−	5

Problem Solving • Reasoning

9. **Write About It** The play started at this time. It lasted 4 hours. What time did it end? Explain.

_____

Name _____ Date _____

Subtract Two-Digit Numbers

Use a workmat with ⬚⬚⬚⬚ and ▢.
Write each difference. Remember to start with
the ones.

1.
Tens	Ones
6	8
− 2	3
4	5

2.
Tens	Ones
2	3
− 1	2

3.
Tens	Ones
7	5
− 5	2

4.
Tens	Ones
6	3
− 2	2

5.
Tens	Ones
3	4
− 1	1

6.
Tens	Ones
5	9
− 2	5

7.
Tens	Ones
4	4
− 3	1

8.
Tens	Ones
3	0
− 1	0

9.
Tens	Ones
7	6
− 6	4

10.
Tens	Ones
9	0
− 3	0

11.
Tens	Ones
5	8
− 2	6

12.
Tens	Ones
8	6
− 2	1

Problem Solving • Reasoning

13. Write a number sentence that shows
two numbers with a difference of fifty.

_____ ◯ _____ = _____

Name _____ **Date** _____

Different Ways to Subtract

Choose a way to subtract. Write each difference.

1.
Tens	Ones
6	9
– 4	2
2	7

2.
Tens	Ones
4	7
– 2	2

3.
Tens	Ones
7	8
– 3	6

4. 34
  – 13

5. 76
  – 41

6. 56
  – 32

7. 86
  – 43

8. 64
  – 3

9. 55
  – 23

10. 98
  – 26

11. 45
  – 32

12. 89
  – 18

13. 28
  – 17

14. $80 - 20 =$ ____ 15. $52 - 2 =$ ____ 16. $46 - 20 =$ ____

Problem Solving • Reasoning

17. Jack had 40 stamps in one book and 50 stamps in another book. He gave 20 stamps to Amy. How many stamps does he have now?

____ stamps

Draw or write to explain.

Name _____   Date _____

Practice Two-Digit Subtraction

Subtract.

1. $\begin{array}{r} 88 \\ -58 \\ \hline 30 \end{array}$	2. $\begin{array}{r} 96 \\ -84 \\ \hline \end{array}$	3. $\begin{array}{r} 74 \\ -12 \\ \hline \end{array}$	4. $\begin{array}{r} 84 \\ -32 \\ \hline \end{array}$	5. $\begin{array}{r} 94 \\ -31 \\ \hline \end{array}$
6. $\begin{array}{r} 78 \\ -55 \\ \hline \end{array}$	7. $\begin{array}{r} 64 \\ -13 \\ \hline \end{array}$	8. $\begin{array}{r} 55 \\ -24 \\ \hline \end{array}$	9. $\begin{array}{r} 74 \\ -52 \\ \hline \end{array}$	10. $\begin{array}{r} 75 \\ -22 \\ \hline \end{array}$
11. $\begin{array}{r} 85 \\ -43 \\ \hline \end{array}$	12. $\begin{array}{r} 76 \\ -43 \\ \hline \end{array}$	13. $\begin{array}{r} 86 \\ -71 \\ \hline \end{array}$	14. $\begin{array}{r} 58 \\ -47 \\ \hline \end{array}$	15. $\begin{array}{r} 62 \\ -41 \\ \hline \end{array}$
16. $\begin{array}{r} 87 \\ -31 \\ \hline \end{array}$	17. $\begin{array}{r} 68 \\ -54 \\ \hline \end{array}$	18. $\begin{array}{r} 95 \\ -34 \\ \hline \end{array}$	19. $\begin{array}{r} 44 \\ -12 \\ \hline \end{array}$	20. $\begin{array}{r} 21 \\ -11 \\ \hline \end{array}$

Problem Solving • Reasoning

21. Andy has 45 sheets of paper. He uses
    12 of them for his homework. How many
    sheets of paper does he have left?

    _____ sheets of paper

Name _____ **Date** _____

Algebra Readiness: Check Subtraction

Subtract. Check by adding.

1. 78
   −34
   ‾‾‾‾
   44   →   44
             +34
             ‾‾‾
             78

2. 85
   −32
   ‾‾‾‾   ☐
            +☐
            ‾‾
            ☐

3. 26
   − 4
   ‾‾‾‾   ☐
            +☐
            ‾‾
            ☐

4. 54
   −43
   ‾‾‾‾   ☐
            +☐
            ‾‾
            ☐

Problem Solving • Reasoning

5. How many fewer peanut butter and jelly sandwiches are there than pizzas?

   ____ fewer sandwiches

6. **Write Your Own** Write a question about this table. Then solve.

School Lunches	
Food	Number
Pizza	46
Grilled Cheese	33
Peanut Butter and Jelly	21

Name _____   Date _____

Add and Subtract Money

Add or subtract.

1. $\begin{array}{r} 49¢ \\ -22¢ \\ \hline 27¢ \end{array}$ 2. $\begin{array}{r} 86¢ \\ +12¢ \\ \hline ¢ \end{array}$ 3. $\begin{array}{r} 38¢ \\ -21¢ \\ \hline ¢ \end{array}$ 4. $\begin{array}{r} 18¢ \\ -12¢ \\ \hline ¢ \end{array}$ 5. $\begin{array}{r} 41¢ \\ -11¢ \\ \hline ¢ \end{array}$

6. $\begin{array}{r} 32¢ \\ +47¢ \\ \hline ¢ \end{array}$ 7. $\begin{array}{r} 95¢ \\ -14¢ \\ \hline ¢ \end{array}$ 8. $\begin{array}{r} 37¢ \\ +61¢ \\ \hline ¢ \end{array}$ 9. $\begin{array}{r} 61¢ \\ +30¢ \\ \hline ¢ \end{array}$ 10. $\begin{array}{r} 99¢ \\ -40¢ \\ \hline ¢ \end{array}$

11. $\begin{array}{r} 63¢ \\ -41¢ \\ \hline ¢ \end{array}$ 12. $\begin{array}{r} 23¢ \\ +13¢ \\ \hline ¢ \end{array}$ 13. $\begin{array}{r} 75¢ \\ -32¢ \\ \hline ¢ \end{array}$ 14. $\begin{array}{r} 17¢ \\ +20¢ \\ \hline ¢ \end{array}$ 15. $\begin{array}{r} 79¢ \\ +10¢ \\ \hline ¢ \end{array}$

Problem Solving • Reasoning

16. **Write About It** Ron has these coins. He wants to buy a coloring book for 25¢. Does he have enough money? Explain.

_____

Name _____   **Date** _____

Count On, Count Back

Count on or count back.

1	2	3	4	5	6	7	8	9	10
11	12	13	14	15	16	17	18	19	20
21	22	23	24	25	26	27	28	29	30
31	32	33	34	35	36	37	38	39	40
41	42	43	44	45	46	47	48	49	50
51	52	53	54	55	56	57	58	59	60
61	62	63	64	65	66	67	68	69	70
71	72	73	74	75	76	77	78	79	80
81	82	83	84	85	86	87	88	89	90
91	92	93	94	95	96	97	98	99	100

1. $39 + 5 =$ _____

2. $69 + 7 =$ _____

3. $86 - 7 =$ _____

4. $33 - 5 =$ _____

5. $44 + 8 =$ _____

6. $28 - 6 =$ _____

7. $42 - 5 =$ _____

8. $75 - 7 =$ _____   9. $65 + 5 =$ _____   10. $95 + 4 =$ _____

Problem Solving • Reasoning

Do you add or subtract? Write + or −.

11. $64 \bigcirc 7 = 57$ 12. $25 \bigcirc 6 = 19$

13. $88 \bigcirc 3 = 91$ 14. $29 \bigcirc 9 = 38$

Name _____   Date _____

Problem Solving: Multistep Problems

Solve. Decide which operation to use first.
Decide which operation to use next.

1. Bart has 20 blue jacks
and 5 red jacks. He
picks up 10 jacks. How
many jacks are left?

   Think: Do I add
   or subtract first?

   Draw or write to explain.

   _____ jacks

---

2. Sam has 29 boxes of
crayons. He passes
out 7 boxes to the
first row of children.
Then he passes out 10 boxes to the second
row of children. How many boxes of
crayons does Sam have left?

   Think: How many
   boxes of crayons
   are there in all?

   Draw or write to explain.

   _____ boxes of crayons

Solve. Choose a strategy.

• Draw a picture.
• Write a number sentence.
• Use models to act it out.

3. Val answers 8 questions on the first
page. She answers 4 questions on
the second page. There are 25 questions
in all. How many questions does Val have
left to answer?

   Draw or write to explain.

   _____ questions